Setting the Stage for Learning

Setting the Stage for Learning

Activating the Power of Stories to Facilitate Learning

William A. Sommers
Lindsey Pollock
Margie Blount
Elita Driskill

ROWMAN & LITTLEFIELD
Lanham • Boulder • New York • London

Published by Rowman & Littlefield
An imprint of The Rowman & Littlefield Publishing Group, Inc.
4501 Forbes Boulevard, Suite 200, Lanham, Maryland 20706
www.rowman.com

86-90 Paul Street, London EC2A 4NE, United Kingdom

Copyright © 2025 by William A. Sommers

All rights reserved. No part of this book may be reproduced in any form or by any electronic or mechanical means, including information storage and retrieval systems, without written permission from the publisher, except by a reviewer who may quote passages in a review.

British Library Cataloguing in Publication Information Available

Library of Congress Cataloging-in-Publication Data

Names: Sommers, William A., author. | Pollock, Lindsey, author. | Blount, Margie, author. | Driskill, Elita, author.
Title: Setting the stage for learning : activating the power of stories to facilitate learning / William A. Sommers, Lindsey Pollock, Margie Blount, Elita Driskill.
Description: Lanham : Rowman & Littlefield, [2025] | Includes bibliographical references and index. | Summary: "Busy leaders and trainers can use the many resources in Setting the Stage for Learning: Activating the Power of Stories to Facilitate Learning to increase impact and readiness for important topics"— Provided by publisher.
Identifiers: LCCN 2024025770 (print) | LCCN 2024025771 (ebook) | ISBN 9781475869545 (cloth) | ISBN 9781475869552 (paperback) | ISBN 9781475869569 (epub)
Subjects: LCSH: Storytelling in education. | Team learning approach in education. | Professional learning communities.
Classification: LCC LB1042 .S65 2025 (print) | LCC LB1042 (ebook) | DDC 372.67/7044—dc23/eng/20240708
LC record available at https://lccn.loc.gov/2024025770
LC ebook record available at https://lccn.loc.gov/2024025771

∞™ The paper used in this publication meets the minimum requirements of American National Standard for Information Sciences—Permanence of Paper for Printed Library Materials, ANSI/NISO Z39.48-1992.

*To Walter (Skip) Olsen who passed away on January 1, 2021. Skip was William (Bill) A. Sommers' partner in producing books and hosting Learning Omnivores events, and was a co-presenter at local, state, and national organizations. Bill misses his counsel, system thinking, and most of all his friendship.
We were an amazing team and I miss him.
Peace to you, Skip.
I love you.*

Contents

Preface	ix
Acknowledgments	xi
Introduction	xiii
1 Courage	1
2 Communication	17
3 Collaboration	33
4 Coaching	47
5 Change	63
6 Conflict	77
7 Creativity	89
8 Conclusion: Give 'em "L" (Leadership)	99
Appendix: Three Things to Know About Copyright Laws When Using Video	105
Contact Information	111
Index	113
About the Authors	115

Preface

"If history were taught in the form of stories, it would never be forgotten."

—Rudyard Kipling

If you think about it, how did the histories of indigenous cultures survive thousands of years? In the past, many cultures on nearly every continent North America, Africa, South America, Europe, Australia, and Asia operated on the basis of proverbs and stories passed down through generations. None of these cultures had three-ring binders sitting on the shelf to guide customs and traditions. The oral proverbs and stories became the social mores and behavioral expectations that provided the community's structure. Stories helped organize communities and create possibilities.

Today, organizations are rediscovering the importance of storytelling to shape organizational cultures and realize possibilities. At Menlo Innovations, Ann Arbor, Michigan, Richard Sheridan's title is CEO and Chief Storyteller. In the opening of *Joy, Inc.* (2013), Dr. Sheridan tells the story of Pierpont Langley who was well financed and hired the experts in order to build a flying machine. He covered every detail. At the same time as Langley was pursuing the dream of flight, there was a group of people organized by the Wright Brothers. They didn't have a lot of money or expertise. They wanted to fly and effectively sold their story to people who could support their dream. Stories and vision can motivate people to accomplish many things. As many writers have said, "If you always do what you did, you always get what you got." Stories can help us dream of a better future.

Stories. When organizing groups and working with individual leaders, telling stories of what has been or what is possible can deliver amazing results. Think of the famous American orators and visionaries who worked for radical change in the 1960s. Dr. Martin Luther King Jr. was a powerful storyteller who helped the nation see a world of possibility where children could someday learn and live together regardless of the color of their skin. Former President John F. Kennedy led the nation to dream of stepping foot on the moon and serving our country in future endeavors. Who remembers his famous line, "We choose to go to the moon in this decade and do the other things, not because they are easy, but because they are hard."

Many of the best staff developers, trainers, and presenters tell stories. While many professionals walk away forgetting the facts (data and tables that flashed on the screen), they walk away remembering the stories that were told. Why?

Generally, stories create emotion and relevance. Brain research tells us that emotion is key to retaining information. Relevance, too, can increase retention and the ability to draw on long-term memory to apply to new or similar problems.

Videos. Visual examples are powerful ways to set the stage for discussion. Therefore, we have also supplied clips and short videos to help focus on topics quickly, sometimes with humor. Teeing up a topic effectively can save time and engage the visual sense.

Quotes. We have found that quotes, metaphors, and proverbs can support retention and refocus the goals of meetings and workshops.

> "Metaphors have a way of holding the most truth in the least space."
> —Orson Scott Card, *Alvin Journeyman*

Activities. The authors know how busy practitioners are, so we have included an activity for use with groups. We hope this helps during those busier than normal times to prepare ahead of time.

References and Suggestions for Further Study. "Where did this come from?" "What can we do next to deepen our understanding?" These are two questions that usually come up in group meetings or an individual. We have provided some additional resources to address these questions and provide background information.

Acknowledgments

Bill recognizes several people who have contributed to his growth as a learner, leader, and leadership coach. This is not an exhaustive list by any means.

Art Costa who started me on a learning journey that I could never have imagined. Our ongoing conversations continue to inspire me. I love you.

Frank Wagner, as the co-developer of Stakeholder Centered Coaching, continues to be gracious with ongoing support, practical ideas, and monthly phone calls sharing his experience and skillful actions with the SCC community.

Michael Ayers who is my go-to guru when trying to make connections of information from different sources and systems thinking. I was fortunate to have him as a parent at South High School. I continue to learn from him every chance I get.

Betty Burks and Laura Robinson who have been great collaborators as we move SCC into the educational field. We believed SCC could change school leadership for the better and it has. Can't wait to see how we increase SCC in education.

Richard Sheridan at Menlo Innovations who gives me hope for making joy a reality in schools. Rich provides a joyful workplace which marries production and humanity. After reading his book, I took a trip to Ann Arbor to see if it could be true. It was and I got more than I expected. What a gift.

Jim Knight who continues to provide instructional improvement for educators, allowing me to present each year at the TLC conference, and keeps recommending books. Then, I read them and learn. You are a great learning partner.

Kim Penny, the technology guru, aka "solutions engineer," who puts up with me because I was born on another planet. Not sure which one, but it wasn't this one. I am in your debt for your flexibility and "can do" attitude.

Marney Wamsley, the principal who kept me in education when I was ready to quit. I am forever grateful. Marney has since passed away in February 2024.

Thank you to Tom Koerner, Jasmine Holman, April Snider, Jessica Smith, and the Rowman & Littlefield family for having the confidence to support this project. Their direction, guidance, and support continue to be extremely helpful.

A special thanks to Lindsey, Margie, and Elita for making this book a better resource for busy leaders. I am grateful for their passion and input.

Lindsey thanks her mother for always looking out for her and modeling that it is never too late to follow your dreams. She thanks her family and friends for their support and patience with her ever busy schedule and desire to do "just one more thing"! She'd also like to thank her children Aaron and Ashley for listening to endless hours of "books on tape" during many long road trips together! She thanks her husband Bobby for his love and encouragement. Lindsey thanks her colleagues and friends at Sarasota University, Center for Guided Montessori Studies and the International Montessori Council for exemplifying all that is possible and right in the world. You have given peace, love, joy, and hope. May you be equally blessed. Finally, Lindsey thanks her co-authors, Bill for sharing his limitless knowledge, wisdom, and compassion, Margie for her dedication and relentless pursuit of excellence and passion, and Elita for her eye for detail and collaborative spirit. They are truly blessings—angels here on earth!

Margie expresses her sincere gratitude to the many leaders who have helped shape her career. She thanks her family and friends for encouraging her to pursue her dreams. Her daughter—Shykeitha, grandson—Ayden, and niece—Deundra are the sources of her inspiration. She thanks Lindsey and Bill, for sharing their knowledge and creativity.

Elita thanks her mother, Sue Martin, who believed she could do or become anything. Her unwavering belief provided a firm foundation for a life filled with love, laughter, and adventure. She also thanks her husband, Dale Driskill, for providing endless support, encouragement, time, and resources to accomplish each dream. He never wavers in his love and patience. Additionally, Elita thanks Bill Sommers, fellow coach and learner, for taking time to listen and provide a pathway to contribute to this project. Thank you for the wonderful learning opportunity and valuable collaboration.

Introduction

"Our goal in life is to gather all the awareness one can, and then to pass it out freely to those who are interested."

—Manitonquat, Keeper of the Lore for the Assonet band of Wampanoag Nation

WHY THIS BOOK?

First, this is a companion book to an earlier publication by Rowman & Littlefield titled *Compliance Cop to Culture Coach* written by Bill Sommers and Jakub Grzadzielski. This book provides stories, videos, activities, references, quotes, and contextual thoughts that complement chapters in the first book. We, the four authors, want to *save you time*. For leaders, time is the most precious renewable resource.

Second, in his recent book *The Performance Paradox: Turning the Power of Mindset into Action* (2023), Eduardo Briceño makes the case that we have spent decades focusing on performance (i.e., test scores, etc.). It is time to focus on the *Learning Zone*. Creating systems, a learning zone, for students and staff builds a culture that supports ongoing learning. This is a longer term strategy to compete in a constantly changing world.

"Not learning is bad. Not wanting to learn is worse."

—African Proverb

Third, leaders at all levels are busy with planned and unplanned events. This resource will help you facilitate meetings by providing meaningful activities focused on strategies that can support your school culture. Most of the chapters can be used for all groups in schools including students, where applicable.

> "God so loved stories that he created man [people]."
> —Roland Barth, *Learning by Heart*

All the authors are experienced leaders. We make the following declaration: every story, video, activity, and so on have been used successfully. The rest of the story is that everything has not always worked (truth in packaging). This is the reason we offer multiple ways to facilitate, encourage, and sustain learning. We wish you well on this journey.

WHY STORIES ARE IMPORTANT

> "Stories are easier to remember because stories are how we remember. When facts become so widely available and instantly accessible, each one becomes less valuable. What begins to matter more is the ability to place the facts in context and to deliver them with emotional impact."
> —Daniel Pink

Leaders tell stories, and we add videos, to increase impact, focus conversations, and assist with the retention of knowledge. Kindra Hall's book *Stories that Stick* outlines ways in which organizations can maximize their story. In her words, "In business, those who tell the best stories win. In life, the most important stories are the ones we tell ourselves." As Indigenous cultures learned centuries ago, values and morals that are transmitted through stories are more memorable than only data. People generally make decisions on emotion and what their heart says, then find data to support their decisions. Yes, that can lead to confirmation biases and attribution errors; however, using storytelling can also create spaces for new possibilities and creativity to envision change. Change that can bring out the best in us.

Stories create an open space for people to exchange meanings and beliefs. It helps colleagues reflect on connections to their own lives and organizations. Stories help newcomers understand the norms when joining an organization. Policy manuals are important, but policy manuals don't address every issue. You can't write a rule for every event. School principals, for example, continually navigate challenges with students, staff, parents, and community members that are not in leadership books or policy manuals. Stories and values guide their decisions as they work through these situations.

Phrases from stories can speak volumes in a short space rather than pages of policy. Phrases we learn from stories like "a stitch in time," "an ounce of prevention," and "crying wolf" can help a leader center their thinking and share strategies with others. There is a story about Mary Barra, CEO of General Motors. When she took over, the dress code policy in the contract was pages of rules and directives. She changed the policy to two words: "Dress appropriately." Yes, safety, covering private parts, and how it affects colleagues are part of dressing appropriately. Keeping it simple and illuminating her position with stories focused the team on what was important.

Stories also encourage conversations. Fast Company (2023) published an article by Michelle Buck, saying frequent conversations were the reason for increased productivity and effectiveness. After all, we learn from watching what happens more than a procedure manual. Etienne Wenger (1998) wrote about how insurance customer service representatives learn their job. It is standing up in their cubicle and asking another colleague on how to handle a situation.

Stories help us connect the heart (emotions) and the head (rational thought) while forcing us to solve potential conflicts from information. The pressure of multiple demands and the short timelines can interfere with good long-term thinking. Making a short-term decision with long-term consequences can be devastating. Kahneman (2011) in his book *Thinking Fast and Slow* makes this case clear.

Our goal is to build the individual and organizational capacity to communicate, practice dialogue, and sustain collaborative group processes. Practicing new and different ways of talking to one another helps widen perspectives, incorporate diverse thoughts, and can lead to collaborative problem solving (Olsen & Sommers, 2004). Professional learning needs to be a system-wide effort where everyone supports everyone else, and everyone feels a bit uncomfortable but safe to take courageous steps toward change and improvement.

Some people think stories are for children. We have found that adults can make rich connections from their experience and insights. We remember attending workshops with great ideas and presenters. When returning to the workplace someone would ask what did you learn? Typically we couldn't remember many of the research citations and data. However, we could clearly tell the colleague the stories or videos used at the learning sessions.

Stories offer short learning experiences that are direct, to the point, and speak in metaphor and analogy. Stories are a familiar cultural form. We tell stories to our children, our colleagues, our families, and our community. Welcome to our "story time" where we will share stories that start conversations, ignite questions and curiosity, and create connections.

ORGANIZATION OF CHAPTERS

- Why This Topic?
- Quotes to Start Conversations
- Stories and Discussion Questions
- Videos and Discussion Questions
- Quotes to Promote Thinking and Learning
- Extension Activity
- Summary Questions
    - How do the stories and/or videos help you make the case for _____?
    - What other learnings can be gleaned from these stories/videos?
    - What values do these stories help transmit to the organization?
- Bibliography

You will note that we've included five quotes to start conversations at the beginning of each chapter and ten quotes at the end of each chapter. We encourage you to use the quotes in any or all of the following ways. At the end of each chapter, we've included templates for you to use to make copies of the quotes. Feel free to add your own as well!

Strategies to Use the Quotes

Make copies of the quotes and cut them into strips. Fold the strips and place them in a bowl at your sign-in station/book. Ask staff members to take a quote each day and share/discuss with their colleagues and/or class (if developmentally appropriate).

Make copies of the quotes and cut them into strips. Place quotes in staff mailboxes and encourage staff members to discuss.

Make copies of the quotes and cut them into strips. Place them in a bowl and have staff members take a quote as they arrive for your staff/grade level meeting. Allow time for staff to reflect on the quote. After everyone has arrived and had time to reflect on their quote, ask folks to find someone with the same quote. Gather in pairs or small groups (recommend no more than four in a group) and discuss for 3 minutes. Then switch and find someone with a different quote to discuss.

Use quotes in your newsletters and in common spaces such as your faculty lounge. Lindsey used to introduce a weekly quote in the teacher lounge and encourage staff to write their reflections in marker on the chart paper or bulletin board.

We have worked to ensure that the quotes in this book are representative of diverse voices and perspectives to enrich our learning!

Chapter 1

Courage

"Courage is rightly esteemed the first of human qualities . . . because it is the quality which guarantees all others."

—Winston Churchill

WHY THIS TOPIC?

Whether teaching, leading, or supporting learning, it takes courage to stand up and facilitate an individual or group of people. "Principled leaders solve more problems" (Lee, 2006). Many studies say making a speech is the most undesirable action we do. It is scary to put yourself out there in front of people.

Additionally, in leadership, making decisions that may be unpopular takes courage. Moving from status quo to new ways of performing takes courage. In communities across the nation differences of opinion are causing more conflict. It takes courage to keep values in tact while tackling difficult issues.

Therefore, having the courage to deal with the fear of change, not getting decisions in line with some people, and keeping the focus on building a culture of learning are, at best, hard to do.

Karen Nemeth in *Exchange Leader* (https://www.exchangepress.com/eed/) reminds us that changes in professional behavior, professional practices, and personal reflection takes *courage*. It is important to remember that when we ask educators to engage in professional learning and change the way we do things, it can be unsettling, difficult, and even scary. We are asking them to take a leap of courage and make change happen! Brené Brown and Tonya Ward Singer offer key resources:

- When we ask educators to change a part of their practice, it may seem as though we are telling that what they've been doing was wrong and that the old way is no longer valid. This can feel like an attack on their "professional self-esteem." If we don't have the courage to let go of an old practice, we can't improve. How can leaders help staff feel supported and open about it?
- Brené Brown says, "Integrity is choosing courage over comfort." It can be uncomfortable to learn and try new teaching practices, but that's what is needed for continued growth and professionalism. By working together discomfort can feel more acceptable—"We're in this together."
- Leaders can also support the courage to change by examining the proposed timeline. Do you need more time? More input? Is there buy-in from leaders and coaches—the people who will model the desired behaviors? Do the leaders understand the level of "disruption" that will result?
- Leaders must have the courage to be the lead learners and fully attend workshops, coaching sessions, and implementation reviews. Do they follow up with staff and ensure that the resources and support required are being provided? How is courageous professional growth and learning recognized?

Stories, quotes, and videos can help set the stage to communicate the message of *courage*. As a presenter, facilitator, or leader this concept can be difficult to communicate and inspire others to action. Courage might seem overwhelming or a lofty unattainable goal. A strategically placed story or video can reduce stress, create connections, and enhance the facilitation. Stories followed by paired and small group discussions create personal connections and build on previous experiences. Stories humanize the issues and help people identify with the hope and possibilities that are shared.

QUOTES TO START CONVERSATIONS

"The most common way people give up their power is by thinking they don't have any." —Alice Walker

"The success of every woman should be the inspiration to another. We should raise each other up. Make sure you're very courageous: be strong, be extremely kind, and above all be humble." —Serena Williams

"Life shrinks or expands in proportion to one's courage." —Anais Nin

"We all have ability. The difference is how we use it." —Stevie Wonder

"A single person with a clarity of conscience and a willingness to speak up can make a difference. What are you willing to speak up about?" —Jon Saphier

STORIES

How do you signal values? Stan Slap (2010), in his book *Bury My Heart at Conference Room B,* has this following story. It describes a leader's value of supporting her direct reports and that she has their back. We have used this story when working to enhance and develop courage in a person or team. Florence Taylor is a pseudonym. The message is clear—have courage. You will not be left behind.

Florence Taylor
By Stan Slap

It is a savage yet triumphant personal history, never revealed to most of her friends and certainly never to anyone who works for her. Florence Taylor has decided to tell her story. Florence is a director in her company, and her company is well known. She was reluctant to have it featured in the book and agreed only if I wouldn't use her real name, the name of her company, or the town where this incident occurred. In this one case, I agree. It was the least I could do; Florence herself still bears the scars of this incident, both emotional and physical.

"I grew up in a very small town in the Deep South. There were two schools in our town; the white school and the black school. Since I'm black I went to the black school, which didn't have as many teachers or books or fun things as the white school. But I was a smart little girl and my mother made up for the lack of resources when I got home every day. Before I could go out and play we would sit at the dining room table and she would take down a big old encyclopedia from the shelf and teach me about the world.

"One day I brought home a report card that was so good my mother said, 'I think we can get you into the white school. Do you want to go?' 'Yes!' I said, because I was a smart girl and I wanted to learn. I didn't know that the school district was under a lot of federal pressure to integrate. Our family talked about it and decided that if the school would accept me I would go—as long as my two older brothers transferred with me. My brothers didn't want to go but they loved their little sister and so they agreed. We would be the first black children at the school.

"I had only two dresses and I got to wear my church dress on my first day in school! I was assigned a set in the back next to a little redheaded white girl and I immediately became best friends with her, the way little girls do. When the bell rang for recess I went out to the schoolyard to play with my new friend and her other friends. All of the girls were in the school yard and all of the boys were playing on the football field. A large wire fence separated the two areas. My new friend told me that boys and girls used to play together, but since my two brothers were here now the school had put up the fence to separate the boys from the girls.

"We were playing and screaming and laughing when we heard screaming of a different kind from the edge of the schoolyard. I looked up to see four huge men on horseback with masks on, carrying baseball bats. They were riding right at us. Everyone ran toward the school building. The teachers got there first and locked the doors behind them. As I was running I could hear my brothers yelling my name. They were clawing at the fence, trying to save me, but the fence was too high.

"I was a fast little girl, weighted almost nothing and most of it was legs. I was already almost to the bleacher seats stacked against the wall of the school building. I knew if I could scramble under those bleachers the horses couldn't get to me. I was just about to roll under the seats when I heard a scream I thought I recognized. I turned around and saw that one of the riders had grabbed my new friend by the hair—she had been playing with me— and was holding her a couple of feet off the ground. She was screaming and sobbing.

"I didn't even stop to think. I just turned around and ran at the man on the horse. He was holding my friend on the left side of the horse. This horse was so big and it was sweating and its eyes were wild and glaring at me. It was trying to move around to hit me with its foot. I ran to the man's right side and sunk my teeth into his leg, biting him as hard as I could.

"The good news is that he dropped my friend, but he picked me up instead. He dragged me by my arm across the concrete and two blocks outside the schoolyard. My Sunday dress got torn off. I was bruised all over, the skin on my back and side and left leg was in ribbons and they tell me that I lost a lot of blood. He left me lying in the street but I don't really remember that.

"My mother came to the hospital every day for five weeks. Every day she brought my school lessons and that old encyclopedia and she would help me study the best I could. When I got out, she asked me what I wanted to do. 'I want to go back to the white school and graduate,' I said. And I did.

"I am a grown woman now. I am a successful executive. I am a wife and I am a mother. In this life I have had an opportunity to learn what is most important to me. What is most important to me is loyalty. The little white girl from that school is still my best friend today. I'm not willing to live without loyalty in my life and I'm not willing to have people I care about live without it.

"We have a lot of pressure on our team these days. You're working very hard and we often don't get the cooperation we need from other departments. Things aren't always easy for us and I know that. I know this will change because we will be the ones to change it—I just can't tell you when it will change.

"But I can tell you this: If you are working for me, and you ever get into trouble trying to do the right thing . . . *I'm coming back for you.*"

Discussion Questions

- What connections do you make in this story?
- Have you ever felt "left behind"?
- Who has come back for you?
- How do we support each other in difficult times?
- What examples do you think of when you reflect on courage?

Add your own questions/reflections:

1.
2.
3.
4.
5.

Gabra
Adapted by William Sommers

There is a nomadic culture in Eastern Africa called the Gabra. They live in Kenya near the Chalbi Desert. Even though they live in the desert with limited resources, the Gabra consider their land as a place of freedom and natural resources. Water, although scarce, is adequate if you know where to find it.

There is water for those who know where to look, good grasses and bad grasses, and trees that provide shelter. It is a good land for camels, and their camels define the Gabra.

The Gabra also keep cattle and goats and they may be tended by herders who live as far as 200 miles from their community. The community travels with camels as they meander around the Chalbi Desert. Camels are constantly moving on in search of forage or to get away from their own dung. Camels want to separate from the dung because ticks collect in the dung and make the camels' lives miserable. Sometimes the ticks carry a disease that can be fatal to camels. So the camels must move and the Gabra move with them.

The Gabra try to pick a new site reachable in a day to avoid a night in the open with all their possessions loaded on their camels. Sometimes they move fifty miles or more when necessary. Every eight years they make pilgrimages to their sacred sites in southern Ethiopia, where Gabra men go through the ceremonies that enable them to graduate from one significant age to the next.

Understandably, people become nervous once the decision to move has been made. Women often get up in the middle of the night to begin packing their households. Everything in the household has its place, is packed, and is loaded in a certain order on the camel. All of the packing and loading is done entirely by women. Men handle the camels in case they become unruly and help the women with heavy objects.

Gabra, being flexible and positive about their entire lives in these unending cycles of migration. They truly live off the land. The Gabra love their desert and see it as a supportive environment where people like themselves can live with dignity. They know how to use their land and to conserve its resource. They move even before they are forced to in order to ensure that the land is replenished for the future. They could stay where they are but are cognizant of the area would become overgrazed when the dry season came round again.

They manage their pastures by setting controlled fires to keep the bush from taking over the land. Gabra burn off the bad grasses to allow the good ones to flourish in the ash. They are also careful of trees. Full-grown acacia trees are protected so they regenerate the landscape.

The Gabra have a philosophy of life that can be summed up in their idea of fertility and plenty. The sky god sends rain to bless the earth, makes the grass grow, and ensures that animals and humans have enough to eat and can grow fat.

Not long ago, the Gabra were briefly the victims of well-intentioned experts. While Kenya was still a British colony, the authorities decided to prohibit the Gabra from firing their grasslands in the old-fashioned way. The result was a buildup of deadwood that caused a huge fire that raged out of control and destroyed a large part of the forest on Marsabit Mountain. Since then, the Gabra's own small controlled fires have been looked upon as a useful and intelligent practice. Nowadays Kenyan ranches are using the Gabra combination of camel browsing and range firing to keep the grasslands under control.

The Kenyan government has begun to realize that taking the nomads off the land is not necessarily a wise thing to do. It has become clear that if the deserts of Africa are spreading, it is not because of the nomads and their way of life—for their survival has always depended on cultivating a harmonious relationship with their environment. The fault is more likely to lie in efforts to squeeze the "economic contributions that their governments have a right to expect" out of regions that have traditionally been used by nomadic herders. Such is the legacy of Western-style development thinking. It is often disastrous for indigenous peoples because planners neglect or scorn their knowledge and so belittle one of humankind's greatest attributes—adaptability. Humans can live almost anywhere, given ecological knowledge and the appropriate social relations. The best development planning takes account of both the interests and the expertise of those in the areas to be "developed." Where this is done, indigenous peoples do not suffer needlessly from a "development" in which they have had no say.

Discussion Questions

- When have you acted in silence versus speaking up when something was wrong?
- Were you a bystander or an active in standing up for your values?
- What actions did you take?
- What would you have done now reflecting on the situation?
- What actions can you take now to make amends if needed?
- In what ways is courage reflected in admitting a mistake?

Add your own questions/reflections:

1.
2.
3.
4.
5.

Ernest Shackleton

Ernest Shackleton ran this ad when looking for members for an Antarctic expedition in 1914:

> Men wanted for hazardous journey. Low wages, bitter cold, long hours of complete darkness. Safe return doubtful. Honour and recognition in event of success.

Ernest Shackleton was an example of what courage is and can be. We are facing so many challenges in education and society that we need to invite courageous people into and retain them in leadership roles. When we refer to leadership, we are referring to leadership at *all* levels. While we could go into much more detail, our succinct definition of leadership here is being able and willing to make decisions and take risks for the greater good. We have a *caveat* related to this story of Shackleton: most of this was written in the male voice. Let's admit up front that we need men, women, and diversity at all levels to model courage not only for our peers but also for our young people.

"Children need models more than critics."

—French Proverb

Ernest Shackleton faced many challenges on his daunting adventure. These challenges gave rise to some of the most important leadership lessons and give us a framework for courage that endures to this day.

"The Boss," as his men called him, built success on a foundation of camaraderie, loyalty, responsibility, determination, and—above all—optimism. With this foundation leaders can attract those with similar attributes and create learning cultures, in education and business, that have long-term implications. The expedition was to Antarctica on a ship named the *Endurance*. Educators must ask themselves about their level of endurance and if they have the courage to continue when the "going gets tough."

Shackleton's strategy was the antithesis of the old command-and-control models. His brand of leadership instead values flexibility, teamwork, and individual triumph. He said, "I am a curious mixture with something feminine in me as well as being a man. I hate to see a child suffer, or to be false in any way."

In 1914–1916 Shackleton led the expedition to Antarctica where the crew got trapped during the journey. Shackleton's leadership resulted in bringing the whole crew through this ordeal even though they ran out of food and supplies and were exhausted.

Here are some of the lessons from that journey:

- *Cultivate a sense of compassion and responsibility for others. You have a bigger impact on the lives of those under you than you can imagine.*
- *Once you make a career decision, commit to stick through the tough learning period.*
- *Do your part to help create an upbeat environment at work. A positive and cheerful workplace is important to productivity.*
- *Broaden your cultural and social horizons beyond your usual experiences. Learning to see things from different perspectives will give you greater flexibility in problem solving.*

- *In a rapidly changing world, be willing to venture in new directions to seize new opportunities and learn new skills.*
- *Find a way to turn setbacks and failures to your advantage.*
- *Be bold in vision and careful in planning.*
- *Learn from past mistakes—yours and those made by others. Sometimes the best teachers are the bad bosses and the negative experiences.*
- *Never insist on reaching a goal at any cost. It must be achieved at a reasonable expense, without undue hardship for your staff.*
- *Don't be drawn into public disputes with rivals. Rather, engage in respectful competition. You may need their cooperation someday.*

Italicized portions are direct quotes from the book in the bibliography section.

For a summary of *Shackleton's Way*, see https://learningomnivores.com/what-were-reading/shackletons-way/.

Shackleton's story and other examples of courageous leadership (Rachel Carson, Dietrich Bonhoeffer, Frederick Douglass, and Abraham Lincoln) are found in Nancy Koehn's 2017 book, *Forged in Crisis*.

Discussion Questions

- How does your team respond in times of stress?
- What systems do you have in your organization to pull together?
- Who steps in to lead when times are tough? Why?
- List ten strategies you and your team use to work together. Discuss.

Add your own questions/reflections:

1.
2.
3.
4.
5.

Neal F. Lane said, "Those organizations—be they businesses, schools, colleges and universities, government agencies—that prepare themselves for the unexpected and help to build a sense of community will, in my opinion, become the leaders in the twenty-first century. The same is true for each of us as individuals." If leaders want security only, most organizations will not survive a status quo mentality as customers, society, and individuals continue to change. To quote the Eagles song title, "Get Over It." We add, have the courage to "get on with it."

Courage is stronger when we are able to prepare for the unexpected. As Mary Catherine Bateson (1989) said in her book, "Life is improvisation." Richard Danzig said: "Organizations are a kind of fossil record of what bothered their predecessors." "The issue is not whether they will encounter different types of crises; they will. The issue is whether they will change fast enough to be prepared for those crises when they occur."

As the authors are former high school principals and district leaders, our daily life was improv. It is not what happens to you that determines your skill level, it is how you respond to what happens to you that will provide learning. You can plan and then life happens. You never know who or what will walk through the door. One of the best learnings to prepare a leader is improv classes. Yes, scared to death and step into it. As you review the following videos, we encourage you to reflect on the demands in your role and the courage you demonstrate in your daily practice.

VIDEOS

Courage to Fail (Famous Failures) (1:16 minutes)

https://www.youtube.com/watch?v=5cZh6tYVM2w

When morale is low or a negative belief system creeps into an organization, we can't be successful, we can't wait, we need to intervene. We have used the following video to explicitly identify other successful people who have had bumps in the road on the way to good outcomes. Costa and Kallick (2023), *Habits of Mind*, have written about taking responsible risks as an intelligent behavior. The goal is to model for those we work with that not everything works the first time or multiple times. The video also shows that perseverance and patience are many times required to achieve the desired final outcomes.

Discussion Questions

- What would you do today if you knew you could not fail?
- What lessons have you learned from past failures?
- Share (reflect on) a time when you felt defeated by "failure."
- How did you find the courage to go on?

Add your own questions/reflections:

1.
2.
3.

4.
   5.

Chito (Courage to Care) (9:09 minutes)

https://biggeekdad.com/2015/12/the-hardest-working-man/

People who are neurodiverse or who think differently than we do may open doors to us that we never considered. When we look outside ourselves and consider the world through the eyes of someone else, we may need courage to embrace a viewpoint that challenges our comfort level but expands our awareness. This is why we need to listen to other people. LD used to mean "learning disability." We think LD should mean "learning differently." Chito demonstrates that no matter what the current condition, we can do something that helps to make a difference. We can contribute to others and help make the world a better place. Chito is an example of persistence, efficacy, and courage. We also applaud Chito's community's courage to care.

Discussion Questions

- What values does Chito exhibit that you want to develop in yourself? In others?
- How does the value of courage support collaboration?
- Who is demonstrating courage in this video?

Add your own questions/reflections:

   1.
   2.
   3.
   4.
   5.

What Happens When Things Go Wrong? (8:14 minutes)

https://www.npr.org/2023/02/14/1156984709/in-tehran-forgoing-a-headscarf-is-a-quiet-daring-protest

On February 14, 2023, National Public Radio (NPR) released an article and accompanying podcast on *All Things Considered* that covered the women of Tehran who have decided to engage in a courageous act of forgoing a headscarf after the death of Mahsa Amini. Ms. Amini died in police custody after being apprehended for refusing to wear the state required Hijab in public. Reporters Fatma Tanis, Courtney Dorning, Connor Donevan, and Mary Louise Kelly spoke to women in Iran who were participating in this quiet, daring protest and discussed the risks to their personal safety and the courage they had to band together against overwhelming odds.

Discussion Questions

- What do you wear that signals who you are to others?
- What beliefs/values do you hold that are "non-negotiable"?
- Does courage mean confrontation?
- What does quiet courage mean to you?

Add your own questions/reflections:

1.
2.
3.
4.
5.

QUOTES TO PROMOTE COURAGE

"We do what we have to do so that we can do what we want to do." —Denzel Washington

"A shepherd should smell like his sheep." —Pope John

"For the great achiever it's all about me. For the great leader, it's all about them." —Alan Mullaly

"We must build dikes of courage to hold back the flood of fear." —Martin Luther King Jr.

"I learned that courage was not the absence of fear, but the triumph over it. The brave man is not he who does not feel afraid, but he who conquers that fear." —Nelson Mandela

"What I began by reading, I must finish by acting." —Henry David Thoreau

"Nobody can go back and start a new beginning, but anyone can start today and make a new ending." —Maria Robinson

"Better to do something imperfectly than to do nothing flawlessly." —Robert H. Schuller

"You gain strength, courage, and confidence by every experience in which you really stop to look fear in the face. You must do the thing which you think you cannot do." —Eleanor Roosevelt

"The important thing is to take that first step. Bravely overcoming one small fear gives you the courage to take on the next." —Daisaku Ikeda

Adapted Values Exercise
Based on a workshop by Stan Slap
Expanded version in *Bury My Heart at Conference Room B*

EXTENSION ACTIVITY

What we have found while doing the following exercise is that values become clear for participants. More importantly, others understand why those values are so important to the person, how you got those values, and what influences your behavior. This helps people work together, share where values intersect, and why some differences might get in the way from time to time.

Here are several ways to get a list of values:

- fifty values are in the book by Stan Slap, *Bury My Heart at Conference Room B*
- one hundred values are in the book by Brené Brown, *Dare to Lead*
- one hundred values are on the internet at Developgoodhabits.com

Wherever you get a list to start, make sure you leave space in the activity for a participant to contribute their value and why that may not be on the original list. Please note that we all have many values. The leader of the activity is facilitating a way to get the most important ones for the discussion.

Values Activity

Step One (3 minutes): Review a list. Narrow your top picks from the list. A suggestion:

1. Pick ten values (the easier part)
2. Then reduce it to five
3. Then reduce it to three

Step Two (2 minutes): Write down some examples of how you got those values.

Step Three (5 minutes): Turn to a neighbor or at your table and tell them how you got that final list of three. Take more time if the group size is large.

The goal is for participants to focus on their values, how they got those values, who might have modeled those values, and be able to share to their table groups or work groups.

Here is a list to start with if you are not using a list from above:

1. Accomplishment—Succeeding in reaching goals
2. Advancement—Progress, promotion, improvement
3. Adventure—Taking risks, new experiences
4. Autonomy—Independence, free will
5. Challenge—Overcoming obstacles
6. Compassion—Empathy, tolerance, and understanding of others
7. Competence—Do things well, consistent self-improvement
8. Control—Influence or direct people's behavior, course of events
9. Courage—Testing limits, facing difficulties with resilience
10. Creativity—Imagination, new ways of doing and seeing
11. Equality—Protection of equivalent status, rights, and opportunities
12. Fairness—Equal consideration, value of the greater good
13. Health—Well-being of mind, body, and spirit
14. Impact—Making a difference, changing the world, creating legacy
15. Integrity—Honor, honesty, strength of character
16. Intelligence—Acquiring and applying knowledge
17. Learning—Continuing education and experiences
18. Peace—Calm, centered, free from stress
19. Power—Ability to influence people and conditions
20. Relationships—Connection with others
21. Respect—Fair treatment, valuing individuals for uniqueness of opinion
22. Security—Financial and/or emotional stability
23. Stability—Predictability and steadiness
24. Tradition—Support for known customs and beliefs
25. Wisdom—Application of knowledge and experience

SUMMARY QUESTIONS

- How do the stories and/or videos help you make the case for courage?
- What other learnings can be gleaned from these stories/videos?
- How do these stories/videos connect to your organization's values?

BIBLIOGRAPHY

Abrams, Stacey. (2018). *Lead From the Outside: How to Build Your Future and Make Real Change.* New York: Picador.

Acho, Emmanuel & Tishby, Noa. (2020). *Uncomfortable Conversations with a Black Man.* New York: Flat Iron Books.

Arbinger Institute. (2000). *Leadership and Self-Deception.* San Francisco: Berrett-Koehler.

Arrien, Angeles. (1993). *The Four-Fold Way: Walking Paths of the Warrior, Teacher, Healer, and Visionary.* New York: HarperCollins.

Baumeister, Roy & Tierney, John. (2011). *Willpower.* New York: Penguin.

Brown, Brené. (2018). *Dare to Lead.* New York: Random House.

Brueggemann, Walter. (2013). *Truth Speaks to Power.* Louisville, KY: Westminster John Knox Press.

Duckworth, Angela. (2016). *Grit: The Power and Passion and Perseverance.* New York: Scribner.

Follmi, Danielle & Follmi, Olivier. (2018). *Wisdom: 365 Thoughts from Indian Masters.* New York: Abrams.

Frankl, Viktor. (1959). *Man's Search for Meaning: An Introduction to Logotherapy.* New York: Beacon Press.

Goldrich, Jordan. (2019). *Workplace Warrior: People Skills for the Bullshit Executive.* Austin, TX: Greenleaf.

Horowitz, Ben. (2014). *The Hard Thing About Hard Things.* New York: HarperCollins.

Janove, Jathan. (2017). *Hard-Won Wisdom.* New York: AMACOM Publishing.

Koehn, Nancy. (2017). *Forged in Crisis: The Power of Courageous Leadership in Turbulent Time.* New York: Scribner.

Lee, Gus. (2006). *Courage: The Backbone of Leadership.* San Francisco, CA: Wiley.

Maybury-Lewis, David. (1992). *Millennium: Tribal Wisdom and the Modern World.* New York: Viking Penguin.

McRaven, Admiral William H. (2023). *The Wisdom of the Bullfrog: Leadership Made Simple (But Not Easy).* New York: Hachette.

Morrell, Margot & Capparell, Stephanie. (2001). *Shackleton's Way.* New York: Penguin Putnam Inc.

Slap, Stan. (2010). *Bury My Heart at Conference Room B.* New York: Penguin.

Chapter 2

Communication

"The job of the leader isn't just to make decisions, it's to make sense."

—John Seely Brown

WHY THIS TOPIC?

Communication is key to building effective relationships with stakeholders and sustaining organizational structures. As a school leader, Margie shared this story as she reflected on her experiences as a school principal. Margie met with a parent during an ARD meeting to determine the support the mother's child with autism would need for the upcoming year. The parent made demands that seemed unreasonable, demands the campus simply could not fulfill in the best interest of the child. The meeting became argumentative as the parent continued to insist on the school to fulfill her requests.

Margie was sure they were going to have to table the ARD as it seemed they were nearing an impasse. The meeting took a sudden turn when the parent declared she wanted her son to be able to approach a bus stop without getting shot. She further shared how she feared her son's behavior and large frame could be alarming to people that did not know him. Once Margie heard the parent express the underlying reasons for her concerns, she understood what was driving the mother's demands. By stopping and really listening to the parent, the team was able to collaborate and develop a plan to support the student's social skills and help alleviate the mother's fears.

Communication is the ability to listen to the other person and collaboratively develop a plan based on a desired outcome. Initially the meeting was driven by a perceived power struggle. Once the true purpose was identified, the conversation shifted to solving the problem.

An extremely important issue is how we communicate and implement embracing diversity, inclusivity, and equity. We recommend the resource *Conscious Classrooms: Using Diverse Texts for Inclusion, Equity, and Justice* (2022) by Allison Briceño and Claudia Rodriquez-Mojica. This book will provide you valuable resources and save you *time* by providing useful templates for your use. We need our schools and communities to respond effectively as we continue to be more diverse. Inequity will be a serious issue and impediment to our shared progress if we continue to use historical models and assume they will suffice in a changing world.

The authors, Allison Briceño and Claudia Rodriquez-Mojica, include sections like "Putting It into Perspective" as an important beginning. This chapter highlights some of the rethinking that will be needed in the future.

Other sections in their book, like "Big Idea," "Tools to Try," "Voices from the Field," and our favorite, "Read This," includes specific articles and excerpts to explore, extend, and energize our learning.

In addition, there are templates provided to help assess where we are and what we might consider for the future. These templates are another example of how the book can save valuable time in our collaborative teams. Strategies for communicating with parents, community, and administrators are also part of this important resource.

Madeline Burley-Allen (1995) in her book *Listening* says in communication we spend 40 percent of our time listening; 35 percent of our time speaking; 16 percent of our time reading; and 9 percent of our time writing. As we embark on this reflection on *communication*, we invite you to listen to your inner dialogue as you consider the importance of communication in your practice and how to support effective communication with others.

QUOTES TO START CONVERSATIONS

"The object of education isn't knowledge, it is action." —Herbert Spencer

"The surest way to make someone worry is to tell him not to." —Joe Moore

"Better to trip with your feet than with your tongue." —Zeno

"In teamwork, silence isn't golden, it's deadly." —Mark Sanborn

"When the whole world is silent, even one voice becomes powerful." —Malala Yousafzai

STORIES

Sometimes we get so focused on communicating our important message or content, that we are only in our head space and forget or overlook the importance and opportunity of engaging the heart. There are many factors that impact this and it may depend on the urgency we feel around the information, the time of the year, our personal reflections, and the connections and relationships we have with our audience. It is critical that as leaders we remember that our communications are more effective when we connect with the people with whom we are communicating. Connections are built through shared understanding and the trust we build. One aspect of trust building is showing our gratitude for others and the contributions they make, however big or small. The following story can be emotional and especially now, we need to make sure professionals know we care. By modeling our thanks and showing appreciation to fellow educators, we build bridges over which our communications can effectively travel.

The next story can activate memories from the past *and* illustrate the strength we build by communicating gratitude. In fact, expressing gratitude impacts our physical well-being and in turn how we feel about others. Showing gratitude to others not only activates dopamine (feel good) to the receiver, neuroscientists have found the one who gives gratitude also gets a dose of dopamine. Always communicate humanity to others. It is the only way to pass it on.

Amy Edmondson's research on psychological safety is having positive effects on organizations. To increase trust, caring, and collaboration, psychological safety is paramount. This concept accelerates communication and collaboration among individuals and teams. Look for ways to tell people they are enough, we are grateful for your contributions, and thank you for being part of our team. The following story can change individuals and families and even your organization.

I Wish You Enough
Original story by Bob Perks in *Chicken Soup for the Grieving Soul*

Recently I overheard a father and daughter in their last moments together at the airport. They had announced the plane's departure.

Standing near the security gate, they hugged and the father said, "I love you, and I wish you enough."

The daughter replied, "Dad, our life together has been more than enough. Your love is all I ever needed. I wish you enough, too, Dad."

They kissed and the daughter left. The father walked over to the window where I was seated. Standing there I could see he wanted and needed to cry.

I tried not to intrude on his privacy, but he welcomed me in by asking, "Did you ever say good-bye to someone knowing it would be forever?"

"Yes, I have," I replied. "Forgive me for asking, but why is this a forever good-bye?"

"I am old, and she lives so far away. I have challenges ahead and the reality is—the next trip back will be for my funeral," he said.

"When you were saying good-bye, I heard you say, 'I wish you enough.' May I ask what that means?"

He began to smile. "That's a wish that has been handed down from other generations. My parents used to say it to everyone . . ." He paused for a moment, and looked up as if trying to remember it in detail, and he smiled even more. "When we said, 'I wish you enough,' we were wanting the other person to have a life filled with just enough good things to sustain them." Then turning toward me, he shared the following as if he were reciting it from memory.

I wish you enough sun to keep your attitude bright no matter how gray the day may appear.

I wish you enough rain to appreciate the sun even more.

I wish you enough happiness to keep your spirit alive and everlasting.

I wish you enough pain so that even the smallest of joys in life may appear bigger.

I wish you enough gain to satisfy your wanting.

I wish you enough loss to appreciate all that you possess.

I wish you enough hellos to get you through the final good-bye.

He then began to cry and walked away. They say it takes a minute to find a special person, an hour to appreciate them, a day to love them; but then an entire life to forget them.

Take time to live and to share your gratitude to others.

To all my friends and loved ones, *I wish you enough.*

Discussion Questions

- Who have you been wanting to tell how meaningful they have been in your life?
- What are you waiting for?
- Can you call, write, email today?
- If you feel compelled, send this story to the people you carry with you today. Make a list of the people who have left an indelible imprint on your life. Even if they are deceased, write them a letter. They will know and so will you.

Add your own questions/reflections:

1.
2.
3.
4.
5.

Have you ever had a conversation with another person and walked away secure in the knowledge that you had clearly communicated your message? You might have even written your message down to follow up on your conversation just to be sure. Consider the following "conversation" in the *Bar of Soap Story* below. Have you ever had a similar situation? What could the participants in this scenario have done differently to make their message clear? If you are using this story in an in person setting, consider securing bars of soap and recruit some of your team to enact the story. Seeing the results of this communication in person can really amplify the message of this scenario!

Bar of Soap Story
Adapted by Bill Sommers
Original is from a comedy routine by Shelley Berman

Dear Housekeeping,
Please do not leave any more of those little bars of soap in my bathroom. I brought my own from home. Please remove the six unopened little bars from the shelf under the medicine chest and the other three in the shower soap dish. They are in my way.

Thank you, Room 214

Dear Room 214,
I was a substitute yesterday. The regular housekeeper will be back tomorrow. I removed the little bars as you requested. I did leave three small bars in case you change your mind. My instructions from the management is to leave 3 soaps daily.

Kathy, substitute housekeeping

Dear Housekeeping,
Apparently Pat did not tell you about my note concerning the little bars of soap. When I got back to my room this evening I found 3 more little bars of

soap. I am going to be here in the hotel for two weeks and have brought my own bar of soap so I won't need the additional bars you are leaving in my room. They are in my way. Please remove them.

Room 214

Dear Room 214,
    We are instructed to leave 3 little bars by the management each day. I took the 6 soaps, which were in your way on the shelf and put them in the soap dish where your bath-size bar was. I put the bath-size bar of soap in the medicine cabinet for your convenience. Please let me know if I can be of further assistance.

Your regular housekeeper, Dotty

Dear Room 214,
    The assistant manager informed me this morning that you called him last evening and said you were unhappy with your housekeeping service. I have assigned a new person to your room. I hope you will accept my apologies for any past inconvenience. If you have any future complaints please contact me so I can give it my personal attention. Call extension 1108 between 8am and 5pm. Thank you.

Manager of Housekeeping

Dear Manager,
    It is impossible to contact you by phone since I leave the hotel for business at 7:45am and don't get back before 5:30 or 6pm. That's the reason I called the manager last night. You were already off duty. I only asked if they could do anything about those little bars of soap. The new person you assigned must have thought I was a new check-in today, since they left another 3 bars of hotel soap in my medicine cabinet along with the regular delivery of 3 bars on the bathroom shelf. In just 5 days here I have accumulated 24 little bars of soap. Why are you doing this to me?

Room 214

Dear Room 214,
    Your housekeeper Pat has been instructed to stop delivering soap to your room and remove the soaps. If I can be of further assistance please call extension 108 between 8am and 5pm. Thank you,

Manager of Housekeeping

Communication 23

Dear Hotel Manager,
My bath-size bar of soap is missing. Every bar of soap was taken from my room including my own bath-size bar of soap. I came in late last night and had to call the bellhop to bring me 4 little bars of soap.

Room 214

Dear Room 214,
I have informed our housekeeper of your soap problem. I cannot understand why there was no soap in your room since our housekeepers are instructed to leave 3 bars of soap each time they service a room. The situation will be rectified immediately. Please accept my apologies for the inconvenience.

Assistant manager

Dear Housekeeping,
Who the hell left 54 little bars of soap in my room? I came in last night and found 54 little bars of soap. I don't want 54 little bars of soap. I want my one bar of bath-size soap that I brought with me. Do you realize I have 54 bars of soap in here? All I want is my bath size bar of soap. Please give me back my bath-size bar of soap.

Room 214

Dear Room 214,
You complained of too much soap in your room so I had them removed. Then you complained to the assistant manager that all your soap was missing so I personally returned them. The 24 bars which had been taken and the 3 bars you are supposed to have. Pat did not know I had returned your soaps so they also brought 24 more, plus the 3 daily bars. I don't know where you got the idea this hotel issues bath-size bars of soap. I was able to locate some liquid body wash, which I left in your room.

Housekeeping Manager

Dear Housekeeping Manager,
Just a short note to bring you up-to-date on my latest soap inventory. As of today I possess:

- On the shelf under the medicine cabinet—18 bars of soap in 4 stacks of 4 and 1 stack of 2.
- On the Kleenex dispenser—11 bars of soap in 2 stacks of 4 and 1 stack of 3.
- On the bedroom dresser—1 stack of 3 bars of soap, 1 stack of 4 hotel-size soap, and 8 more bars of soap in 2 stacks of 4.
- Inside the medicine cabinet—14 bars of soap in 3 stacks of 4 and 1 stack of 2.
- In the shower soap dish—6 bars of soap, very moist.
- On the northeast corner of the tub—1 bar of soap, slightly used.
- On the northwest corner of the tub—6 bars of soap in 2 stacks of 3.
- 1 dispenser of liquid bath wash.

Please ask Housekeeping when they service my room to make sure the stacks are neatly piled and dusted. Also, please advise them that stacks of more than 4 have a tendency to tip. May I suggest that my bedroom windowsill is not in use and will make an excellent spot for future soap deliveries. One more item, I have purchased another bar of bath-sized soap which I am keeping in the hotel vault in order to avoid further misunderstandings.

Room 214

Discussion Questions

- What barrier in communication was impeding the successful resolution?
- How do standards of operation sometimes get communicated in ways that seem void of good judgment?
- How would you, as a leader, ensure that communication was improved for an effective resolution?
- The Pareto Principle provides an 80/20 rule: 80 percent of the results come from 20 percent of the processes; 20 percent of the results come from 80 percent of the time and energy. How do you ensure that you have feedback loops of communication to modify procedures that no longer serve the best interest of your organization?
- What results do you use to determine the effectiveness of your communication?

Add your own questions/reflections:

1.
2.

3.
4.
5.

In Dr. Marshall Rosenberg's (2015) book, *Nonviolent Communication: A Language of Life*, he shared that words matter. He emphasized that the four vital components of communication are:

- Consciousness: a set of principles that support living a life of compassion, collaboration, courage, and authenticity.
- Language: understanding how words contribute to connection or distance.
- Communication: knowing how to ask for what we want, how to hear others even in disagreements, and how to move toward solutions that work for all.
- Means of Influence: sharing "power" *with* others rather than using "power" *over* others.

Window & Mirrors
By Bill Sommers

Reflecting on my behavior, and the behavior of others, it occurred that life is a series of windows and/or mirrors.

First, windows. Peter Drucker and Frances Hesselbein often used the question, "When you look out the window, what do you see that others don't see?" Being able to describe what the preferred future is becomes critical for a leader. People in organizations have heard lots of high flatulent language. The better you can describe what you want, the more people will believe you.

Sam Keen (1991), in a book titled *Fire in the Belly,* said everyone has to answer two questions:

1. Where are you going?
2. Who will go with you?

Never get those two out of order.

So, the Drucker/Hesselbein question is extremely important. What do you see and what will be the success indicators that the vision has been accomplished?

Second, mirrors. When you look in the mirror, what do you see? Can you state that you have acted with the best intention and integrity? Did you act according to your values? Of course, I have strayed from my values at times. The mirror reminds me every morning, did I do the right thing? The right decision is not always easy. What is easy is not always right. If you have to choose, choose the right one. It is the best long-term strategy.

Remember, the kids and adults that Marshall Rosenberg is working with are looking for guidance to get on the right path, and that can be very hard depending on the internal and external resources we have.

The mirror also reminds me to reflect-*on*-actions to decide it they are productive. Reflect-*for*-action when planning. However, we all must live in a reflect-*in*-action. That is the daily grind.

Discussion Questions

The story connects Rosenberg's work.

- What are you conscious of when you reflect internally on the past?
- Peter Drucker asked a question: When you look out the window, what do you see that nobody else sees? That is a future.
- If you are not looking in a mirror for reflection or at a window looking at a future, are you seeing a wall?
- What language do you use to project a preferred future?
- How do you communicate that to others?

Add your own questions/reflections:

1.
2.
3.
4.
5.

The Sale Is in the Tale

John Livesay wrote this book in 2022. He reminds us that we rarely buy a product or an idea based on only data. Logical facts can be helpful but we put more credibility in emotions and connections. For instance, if we know someone we trust and they recommend a product or business, we are more likely to seek their advice.

The same holds true when communicating internally with staff or externally with the community. People want to know why they should think or act differently. Connecting with their emotions and providing a preferred future go a long way in developing and sustaining support.

One caveat we have learned about communicating is that colleagues need to know that change is possible. Communicating a vision for the future is critical in telling people why and how we will benefit from a different outcome.

Chip and Dan Heath wrote in *Power of Moments* (2017) how would you create an experience that people will remember 25 years later? How would you create a lesson/workshop/group activity that people would remember in 25 years? This has implications for teachers and leaders. How do you or would create the experience to have the deepest impact and lasting memories? Here are Livesay's five secrets:

Secret 1: The Elevator Story

Is it clear? The fewer words the better. The brain remembers the focus more than lots of information. Giving too much information clouds the memory. Is the story compelling? Use an emotional hook to intensify the amygdala, the emotional center in the brain.

Secret 2: Story of Origin

Why am I doing this job? What drew me to the position? What do I hope to accomplish? John Merrow reported that over 80 percent of the people who go into education want to make a difference.

Secret 3: The Company Story

You can use this template to create your story:

- What do you love about your job?
- Who in your industry inspires you?
- What are the core values of your company (or you)?
- How do you demonstrate those values? A story of the values in action will make it so much more.
- How do you give back to your community?

Secret 4: Case Stories

Give an example of an issue, how you are trying to resolve it, and possible implementation.

Secret 5: Playlist of Stories from Your Experience

Possible topics:

- emotions
- data
- research
- pictures, videos

If you are leading an organization, team, or speaking in public, this book will be invaluable to help you use stories to increase impact.

Discussion Questions

- How do stories, videos, graphics, and visuals increase memory and organize ideas?
- How would you, as a leader, promote using your own knowledge and experience to message direct reports?
- How do you modify or delete procedures that no longer serve the best interest of the students, staff, or community? Make a "to don't list."

Add your own questions/reflections:

1.
2.
3.
4.
5.

VIDEOS

Everybody Loves Raymond (3 minutes)

https://www.youtube.com/watch?v=IqRleb7qRvg

In this clip, Debra and Raymond struggle to understand each other's perspective. Consider these three steps of active listening and how using these steps might positively impact the interaction.

Listening is the receptive component of communication and can be enhanced by consciously focusing on three basic skills: attitude, attention, and adjustment.

Attitude: A positive attitude paves the way for open-mindedness. Assume from the start that you are going to have a positive interaction. Even if the other person says something that makes you wonder, lean in with curiosity instead of judgment.

Attention: Focus on the message you are hearing and allow the words to enter your short-term memory, where they are swiftly processed into ideas. If they aren't processed, then they will be dumped from short-term memory and will be gone forever. Attentive listening makes sure the ideas are processed.

Adjustment: Be flexible enough to follow conversation in whatever direction it may take. Ask clarifying questions and stay present. Your nonverbal message on connectedness helps the other person stay focused and heard.

As you watch this video, consider the questions below.

Discussion Questions

- What is happening in this scenario that is impeding communication?
- What could change to support more effective communication?
- How do you personally communicate with others?
- How do you know your communications are effective?

Add your own questions/reflections:

1.
2.
3.
4.
5.

Story of a Sign Video (5:56 minutes)

https://www.youtube.com/watch?v=e_OcSqrKNGw

Words matter. This video gives an example of making our language visible. We know from research that our language can signal positive presuppositions (when you are successful, what will the students be doing?) or limiting presuppositions (even Bill could get an "A" in that class). Words can change moods, actions, motivations, and so on. Words that match our non-verbal actions are even more powerful.

Discussion Questions

- How did the passerby change the meaning to help get more contributions?
- How can you change the words to get better support for ideas?
- What quotes, metaphors, or proverbs speak to you the most?
- How can you use words to extend meaning and touch the heart as well as the mind?

Add your own questions/reflections:

1.
2.
3.

4.
   5.

Signs (12 minutes)

   https://www.karmatube.org/videos.php?id=1646

   Communication is conveyed in many forms. Communication can be verbal and non-verbal. Here is another example of the power of the written word. What are signs around you communicating? Make your words count, think about the impact of your words before you say them. Seize the day! Spend a day focusing on communicating gratitude and compliments (sincere) to others and watch to see if it impacts *your* mood.

Discussion Questions

- How do you decide what method of communication to use?
- How do you differentiate for your audience?
- How can you share your gratitude with others around you?
- How can you communicate gratitude as part of your daily practice?

Add your own questions/reflections:

   1.
   2.
   3.
   4.
   5.

Communication Problems (7 minutes)

   https://www.youtube.com/watch?v=dBT6u0FyKnc

   Sometimes our messages, both given and received, can be at risk of misinterpretation. In this clip, we see a store clerk and customer struggle to fill the order.

Discussion Questions

- What barriers to understanding have you encountered?
- How do you ensure that the messages you are communicating are clear and understood?

- How do you know you are communicating effectively? Short term? Long term?

Add your own questions/reflections:

1.
2.
3.
4.
5.

QUOTES TO PROMOTE COMMUNICATION

"The single biggest problem in communication is the illusion that it has taken place." —George Bernard Shaw

"Great communication begins with connection." —Oprah Winfrey

"The art of communication is the language of leadership." —James Humes

"The idea is to write it so that people hear it and it slides through the brain and goes straight to the heart." —Maya Angelou

"It's important to make sure that we're talking with each other in a way that heals, not in a way that wounds." —Barack Obama

EXTENSION ACTIVITY

Last Word: An Improv Exercise

People are often thinking about what they want to say before the person they're talking to has finished speaking, missing the latter part of the conversation. This game is designed to help practice staying present in the moment, and listening through to the last word.

Player One makes a statement. Player Two starts another sentence with the last word of Player One's statement. Player Three then starts a sentence with the last word of whatever Player two said, and so on.

SUMMARY QUESTIONS

- How do the stories and/or videos help you "make the case" for communication?
- What other learnings can be gleaned from these stories/videos?
- How do these stories/videos connect to your organization's values?

BIBLIOGRAPHY

Briceño, Allison & Rodriguez-Mojica, Claudia. (2022). *Conscious Classrooms: Using Diverse Texts for Inclusion, Equity, and Justice.* Available at: http://works.bepress.com/allison-briceno/71/.

Burley-Allen, Madelyn. (1995). *Listening: The Forgotten Skill.* New York: John Wiley & Sons.

Godin, Seth. (2003). *Purple Cow.* New York: Penguin Group.

Godin, Seth. (2005). *The Big Moo.* New York: Penguin Group.

Heath, Chip & Heath, Dan. (2017). *The Power of Moments.* New York: Simon & Schuster.

Hoover, Nadine Claire. (2018). *Creating Cultures of Peace: A Movement of Love and Conscience.* Alfred: Conscious Studio.

Livesay, John. (2022). *The Sale Is in the Tale.* Los Angeles: Tradecraft Books.

Olsen, Walter & Sommers, William. (2004). *Trainer's Companion.* Baytown, TX: AHAProcess.

Reason, Casey. (2015). *STOP Leading Like It's Yesterday: Key Concepts for Shaping Today's School Culture.* Bloomington: Solution Tree Press.

Rosenberg, Marshall. (2015). *Nonviolent Communication: A Language of Life.* Encinitas: PuddleDancer.

Sanfelippo, Joe & Sinanis, Tony. (2016). *Hacking Leadership: 10 Ways Great Leaders Inspire Learning That Teachers, Students, and Parents Love.* Highland Heights: Times 10.

Chapter 3

Collaboration

"If there is anything that the research community agrees on, it is this: The right kind of continuous, structured teacher collaboration improves the quality of teaching and pays big, often immediate, dividends in student learning and professional morale in virtually any setting."

—Mike Schmoker, 2004

WHY THIS TOPIC?

As we mentioned in the chapter on communications, no matter where you work or your role in an organization, you will be in collaboration with others. The days of closing your door to your classroom, being in a cubicle, or working by yourself for most of the day are over. Even if you're working from home, you are in connection with other people on your team and accountable to your organization. Collaborative efforts, even via electronic platforms, are needed and are increasing in importance as we navigate the demands of an even more complex and daunting society. While we recognize there are situations that may require solitude for specific tasks like completing budgets, detailed planning, or, most importantly, reflection, leaders report that the majority of time is spent in meetings or connecting with others working on projects. These may be one-on-one, small groups, or large organization-wide endeavors depending upon the scope of the work.

Most innovative companies find ways to have focused productive meetings as opposed to wasting time. Pixar uses a process called "plussing." How do a group of people add suggestions with no trashing of ideas? Rule: Make suggestions to make "it" better.

Menlo Innovations does a process called "Hey Menlo." Fifty plus people gather each day to report on their projects. They use a "Viking" helmet where each two-person team grabs a horn. In about 20 minutes, they go around reporting to everyone the following:

1. What are they working on?
2. What are they learning?
3. Where might they need help?

At the end of the short meeting, teams connect with each other to give ideas based on the team's prior experience. There are other ways to organize meetings. See *Creating Talent Density* (2021) published by Rowman & Littlefield for twenty-five ways to work with teams.

QUOTES TO START CONVERSATIONS

"Mikono mingi kazi haba" which means "Many hands make light work." —Swahili saying

"Cooperation is the thorough conviction that nobody can get there unless everybody gets there." —Virginia Burden

"Unity is strength . . . when there is teamwork and collaboration, wonderful things can be achieved." —Mattie Stepanek

"When you need to innovate, you need collaboration." —Marissa Mayer

"Let us put our minds together and see what life we can make for our children." —Sitting Bull

STORIES

James Surowiecki (2004) in his book, *The Wisdom of Crowds*, studied decisions made by a team compared to decisions made by the smartest person in the room. He found that decisions made by the individual were considered to be 61 percent effective while decisions made by a team were at 91 percent effective. Why? When you have a team, different perspectives are represented, more people are included in the process, and the decisions tend to stay made versus people saying their view wasn't part of the final report. Another byproduct is to have more diverse and inclusionary voices making decisions. So, how do we intentionally include a variety of viewpoints? How do we embrace the mavericks and the alternative thinkers as sources of vital insights and information instead of something to be avoided?

Carol Fulp described the following situation in her 2018 book *Success through Diversity: Why the Most Inclusive Companies Will Win* and why collaboration was key to the breakthrough.

While on a business trip to Kenya, Carol Fulp noticed that a preferred mode of transportation across the country was running. She was amazed to see uniformed school children running to and from school while adults ran to and from work. Some people even engaged in lively discussions as they ran together. Upon her return to the United States, Carol started thinking about the connections to running in her hometown of Boston where the world renowned Boston Marathon, a running event, was held every year. How could she connect running to her work John Hancock Financial Services? Fulp was not a runner herself, but she recognized that this could be a powerful opportunity to offer broad support in her community and leverage the power of her organization's brand. By collaborating with many other people in her organization and other community-based organizations, Fulp was able to bring running and the underlying value of running to a broader audience including the school children of Boston. Her efforts would form the John Hancock Boston Marathon Kenya Project. Elements of the project include hosting marathoners from Kenya to Boston to interact with school children. Kenyan marathoners and John Hancock employees would travel with school children to the African Tropical Forest in the Boston Franklin Zoo where children would learn about the indigenous flora and fauna. Back at school, children would receive lessons about the people of Kenya and learn basic greetings in Swahili. What started off as a business trip to Kenya ended with a popular cross-cultural, international collaboration that benefited thousands of school children.

Discussion Questions

- How do we celebrate differing points of view?
- How do we pursue, accept, and encourage diverse ideas? Or how do we respond when a differing idea challenges us?
- What values and skills do we want to pass on to our children and/or students?

Add your own questions/reflections:

1.
2.
3.
4.
5.

The Whale
Originally published in the *San Francisco Chronicle*

If you read the frontpage story of the *San Francisco Chronicle*, you would have read about a female humpback whale who had become entangled in a spider web of crab traps and lines.

She was weighed down by hundreds of pounds of traps that caused her to struggle to stay afloat. She also had hundreds of yards of rope wrapped around her body, her tail, her torso, and a line tugging in her mouth. A fisherman spotted her just east of the Farralone Islands (outside the Golden Gate) and radioed an environmental group for help. Within a few hours, the rescue team arrived and determined that she was so bad off, the only way to save her was to dive in and untangle her—*a very dangerous proposition.* One slap of the tail could kill a rescuer.

They worked for hours with curved knives and eventually freed her. When she was free, the divers say she swam in what seemed like joyous circles. She then came back to each and every diver, one at a time, and nudged them, pushed them gently around—she thanked them. Some said it was the most incredibly beautiful experience of their lives.

The guy who cut the rope out of her mouth says her eye was following him the whole time, and he will never be the same. *May you, and all those you love, be so blessed and fortunate to be surrounded by people who will help you get untangled from the things that are binding you. And may you always know the joy of giving and receiving gratitude. I pass this on to you in the same spirit.*

Discussion Questions

- When have you been part of a team that accomplished difficult and meaningful results?
- When have you been in the position of the whale needing help?
- How did you thank others for helping you?
- How did collaboration save this whale? What other collaborative efforts are needed to save education? Environment? Next generation? _____?

Add your own questions/reflections:

1.
2.
3.

4.
5.

Collaborating on Our Priorities

"The things that matter most should never be at the mercy of things that matter least."

—Goethe

Do our children matter most? Are kids still in cages? Are children dying because of the constant conflict abroad or here at home? Modeling is the first teacher. Is this what we want to model for our kids? Adults, we have a responsibility here.

Educators are working hard—overworking in many cases—trying to hold on to sanity and prepare students for a future. Many times they are diverted by the multiple demands on them and the system. We sometimes forget why we wanted to go into education.

It is not hard to see that when the demands outweigh the resources, stress continues to increase. As author and Holocaust survivor Viktor Frankl said, "We can live with the how if we know the why." Let's remember the "why."

David Walsh (1994) included a quote from a Cree elder in his book that seems to fit here: "Children are the purpose of life. We were once children and someone cared for us."

We are grateful to Reverend Patrick T. O'Neill for creating this story. It is an important beginning but not an ending. As polarization continues over many issues in our country and the world, we are increasingly concerned that we are losing sight of some of the most important issues of our time. As long-time educators, we see children as a critical resource for our future.

This next story is an example of how a community can keep a major concept in mind during the daily grind. The Masai culture transmits a primary goal through oral communication. As you read the story, you will understand how the important goal is kept alive and distributed through daily conversations. The Masai culture has it right. Let's learn from them.

"How Are the Children?"
Excerpt from a speech by Reverend Patrick T. O'Neill

Among the many accomplished and fabled tribes of Africa, no tribe was considered to have warriors more fearsome or more intelligent than the mighty Masai. It is perhaps surprising then to learn the traditional greeting that passed between Masai warriors. "Kasserian Ingera," one would always say to another. It means "And how are the children?"

It is still the traditional greeting among the Masai, acknowledging the high value that the Masai place on their children's well-being. Even warriors with no children of their own would always give the traditional answer, "All the children are well." This meant, of course, that peace and safety prevail; that the priorities of protecting the young and the powerless are in place; that the Masai people have not forgotten their reason for being, their proper function, and their responsibilities. "All the children are well" means that life is good. It means that the daily struggles of existence, even among poor people, include the proper care of the young and defenseless.

I wonder how it might affect our consciousness or our own children's welfare if, in our own culture, we greeted each other with the same daily question, "And how are the children?" I wonder if we heard that question and passed it along to each other a dozen times a day if it would begin to make a difference in the reality of how children are thought of or cared for in this country?

I wonder what it would be like if every adult among us—parents and non-parents alike—felt an equal weight of responsibility for the daily care and protection of all the children in our town, in our state, in our country. I wonder if we could truly say without hesitation, "The children are well; yes, all the children are well."

What would it be like? If the president began every press conference, every public appearance, by answering the question: "And how are the children, Mr. President?" If every governor of every state had to answer the same question at every press conference: "And how are the children, Governor? Are they well?" Wouldn't it be interesting to hear their answers?

Discussion Questions

- How are our children?
- What are positive actions that support and guide our children?
- What are potholes, barriers, or "rocks in the road" preventing us from unleashing children's potential?
- How do we collaborate with children?
- How do we understand the child's point of view?
- How are the educators?

Add your own questions/reflections:

1.
2.
3.
4.
5.

The Collaboration Cycle

Many organizations go through cycles of ups and downs. Looking at the work of Lawrence Miller (1989), *Barbarians to Bureaucrats*, the typical cycle is: A prophet comes up with an idea, the barbarians engage people and implement the idea. A manager takes over to institutionalize the product of the process. Enter the bureaucrat. Nothing changes but the results are dwindling. The aristocracy, who have benefitted from the initial innovation, start hiring people to protect them. See the link below for a more complete summary of the book:

https://learningomnivores.com/what-were-reading/barbarians-to-bureaucrats/

The Monk's Story
Adapted by Bill Sommers
Original from *The Art of Possibility* by Rosamund Stone Zander and Benjamin Zander

A Monastery had fallen on hard times. It was once a vibrant order but as a result of religious persecution in the seventeenth and eighteenth centuries and the rise of secularism in the nineteenth century, almost all its community houses were lost. The order had become decimated to the extent that there were only five monks left in the decaying mother house, the abbot and four others, all over seventy in age. Clearly it was a dying order.

In the deep woods surrounding the monastery there was a little hut that a rabbi from a nearby town occasionally used for seclusion, reflection, and contemplation. Through many years of prayer and contemplation, the old monks had become a bit psychic. They could sense when the rabbi was in the hermitage. "The rabbi is in the woods, the rabbi is in the woods again," they would whisper to each other. As the abbot agonized over what to do about the decline of his order, the abbot decided to visit the heritage and ask the rabbi if he could offer any advice that might save the monastery.

The rabbi welcomed the abbot at his hut. When the abbot explained the purpose of his visit, the rabbi could only commiserate with him. "I know how it is," he exclaimed. "The spirit has gone out of the people. It is the same in my synagogue." So, the old rabbi and the old abbot wept together. They read parts of the Torah and quietly spoke of deep things. When the time came for the abbot to leave, they embrace each other. "It has been a wonderful thing that we should meet after all these years," the abbot said, "but I have still failed in my purpose for coming here. Is there nothing you can tell me, no piece of advice you can give me that would help me save my dying order?"

"No, I am sorry," the rabbi responded, "I have no advice to give. The only thing I can tell you is that the Messiah is one of you."

When the abbot returned to the monastery the fellow monks gathered around him to ask, "Well, what did the rabbi say?"

"He couldn't help," the abbot answered. "The only thing he did say, just as I was leaving—it was something cryptic—was that the Messiah is one of us. I don't know what he meant."

As they contemplated and considered the message the Rabbi said, the old monks began to treat each other with extraordinary respect, on the off chance that one of them might be the Messiah. And on the off chance that each monk himself might be the Messiah, they began to treat themselves with extraordinary respect.

"The Messiah is one of us? One of us, here, at the monastery? Do you suppose he meant the Abbot? Of course, it must be the Abbot. He has been our leader for so long. On the other hand, he might have meant Brother Thomas, who is certainly a holy man. Or could he have meant Brother Elrod, who is so crotchety? But then Elrod is very wise. Surely, he could not have meant Brother Phillip—he is too passive. But then, magically, he's always there when you need him. Of course, he did not mean me, or suppose he did? Oh Lord, not me! I could not mean that much to you, could I?"

Because the forest in which it was situated was beautiful, people occasionally came to visit the monastery, to picnic or to wander along the old paths, most of which led to the dilapidated chapel. They sensed the aura of extraordinary respect that surrounded the five old monks. They began to come more frequently, bringing their friends, and their friends brought friends. Some of the younger men who came to visit began to engage in conversation with the monks. After a while, one asked if he might join. Then another, and another. Within a few years, the monastery became once again a thriving order, thanks to the Rabbi's gift. A vibrant, authentic community and love for the whole realm.

Discussion Questions

- What do you think were some of the behaviors the monks did to change the order?
- What were the reflective thoughts that can change our focus and attitude?
- What could the abbot, as the leader, do to encourage collaboration?

Add your own questions/reflections:

1.
2.
3.
4.
5.

VIDEOS

Turtles (1 minute)

https://www.youtube.com/watch?v=pUyuk6kbssQ

Collaboration takes place in the "wild"! In this video, we find a turtle in a pool on its back. Several other turtles surround the struggling turtle to help it get right-side up. Do turtles know something we don't?

Discussion Questions

- Have you ever been on your back trying to get upright?
- What helped? What hindered?
- Who helped you the most?
- Have you told them "thank you"?

Add your own questions/reflections:

1.
2.
3.
4.
5.

Together We're Better (30 seconds)

https://www.youtube.com/watch?v=sNZk4ji95hQ

An example of collaboration is central in this video when one lone crab is vulnerable. All by itself, the crab might be dinner to a bird killing and eating the crab. When the crabs come together, they are able to withstand the attack by the bird. What is your team coming together around? Are there internal/external factors that can be more effectively handled with a collaborative approach?

Discussion Questions

- Have you ever been alone and seen an impending disaster ahead?
- What did you do to protect or avoid the negative consequences?
- Who or how many came to the rescue?

Add your own questions/reflections:

1.
2.
3.
4.
5.

Declaration of Interdependence (4 minutes)

https://www.karmatube.org/videos.php?id=4246

Filmmaker Tiffany Shlain rewrote the U.S. Declaration of Independence to be A Declaration of Interdependence and asked people all over the world to film themselves reading the script and send in the videos. Video, art, and translation submissions poured in from all over the world in over fifty languages, helping to pioneer "cloud filmmaking." Watch this exhilarating montage of user-generated content demonstrating the vast potential of creative collaboration.

Discussion Questions

- What kind of thinking brings people together for a better result for common safety?
- What outside threat would be enough for an organization to come together?
- How do we build groups to withstand outside threats?

Add your own questions/reflections:

1.
2.
3.
4.
5.

QUOTES TO PROMOTE COLLABORATION

"Teamwork is so important that it is virtually impossible for you to reach the heights of your capabilities or make the money that you want without becoming very good at it." —Brian Tracy

"Creating a better world requires teamwork, partnerships, and collaboration as we need an entire army of companies to work together to build a better world within the next few decades. This means corporations must embrace the benefits of cooperating with one another." —Simon Mainwaring

"We talk a lot about hope, helping, and teamwork. Our whole message is that we are more powerful together." —Victoria Osteen

"If you're going to preach dedication, work ethic, teamwork, unselfishness, and being part of a team to accomplish a common goal, you have to live it—you can't just talk about it." —Chris Mullin

"When employees join executives in truly owning the responsibility for business success, an exciting new sense of teamwork takes hold." —Punit Renjen

"I'm a true believer in the strength of teamwork, in the power of dreams, and in the absolute necessity of a support structure." —Julie Payette

"Service people are capable. They gain world-class professional skills while in uniform. They use those skills in the most challenging places, showing the kind of teamwork and leadership most of us can only dream of." —Anna Soubry

"I like people who are working on practical things and who are working in teams. It's not so important to get the glory. It's much more important to get something that works. It's a better way to live." —Freeman Dyson

"On great teams—the kind where people trust each other, engage in open conflict, and then commit to decisions—team members have the courage and confidence to confront one another when they see something that isn't serving the team." —Patrick Lencioni

"Collaboration is a key part of the success of any organization, executed through a clearly defined vision and mission and based on transparency and constant communication." —Dinesh Paliwal

EXTENSION ACTIVITY

Figure 3.1 is from the book *The Ideal Team Player* by Patrick Lencioni. The three elements for an effective team player is being smart, hungry, and humble:

- There are many ways to be smart. One of the best indicators is to assess whether the person is intellectually curious and has the horsepower to find research about a given subject.
- To be hungry means wanting to understand better, to make a larger contribution, or to move into a leadership position. Hungry for learning would be a great way to assess value to the team.
- Being humble can sometimes be a problem. In coaching others, if a leader knows everything, there is nothing for a coach to add. As Marshall Goldsmith says, "There must be a desire to improve a skill or get better at something."

Search your browser for "Ideal Team Player." Choose an image. Share with the team to assess where individuals reside, where they want to be, and strategies to move toward the center.

Questions to ponder based on the graphic for individuals and teams to improve:

1. Assess where you reside.
2. Assess where your teammates reside.
3. What would it take to have more colleagues occupy the middle overlap of the Venn diagram?

SUMMARY QUESTIONS

- How do the stories and/or videos help you make the case for collaboration?
- What other learnings can be gleaned from these stories/videos?
- How do these stories/videos connect to your organization's values?

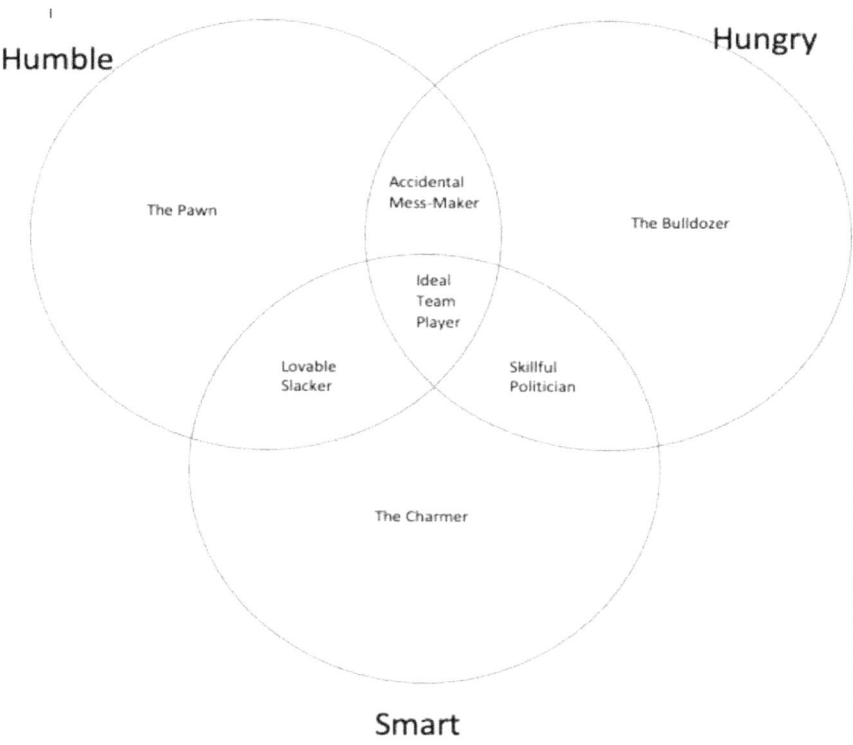

Figure 3.1. Ideal Team Player Diagram.

BIBLIOGRAPHY

"And How Are the Children?" (2015). WorshipWeb. www.uua.org. January 21, 2015. https://www.uua.org/worship/words/reading/and-how-are-the-children.

Andreola, Karen. (2002). *Pocketful of Pinecones: Nature Study with the Gentle Art of Learning—A Story for Mother Culture.* Union, ME: Charlotte Mason Research & Supply.

Block, Peter. (2009). *Community: The Structure of Belonging.* San Francisco: Berrett-Koehler Publishing, Co.

Daleo, Morgan. (1996). *Curriculum of Love: Cultivating the Spiritual Nature of Children.* Charlottesville, VA: Grace Publishing & Communications.

Drago-Severson, Eleanor & Blum-DeStefano, Jessica. (2016). *Tell Me So I Can Hear You.* Cambridge, MA: Harvard Education Press.

Edmondson, Amy. (2012). *Teaming.* San Francisco: Jossey-Bass.

Fulp, Carol. (2018). *Success through Diversity: Why the Most Inclusive Companies Will Win.* Boston, MA: Beacon Press.

Hargreaves, Andy & O'Connor, Michael. (2018). *Collaborative Professionalism.* Thousand Oaks: Corwin Press.
Lencioni, Patrick. (2005). *Overcoming the Five Dysfunctions of a Team.* San Francisco: Jossey-Bass.
Lencioni, Patrick. (2016). *The Ideal Team Player.* Hoboken, NJ: Wiley & Sons.
Miller, Lawrence. (1989). *Barbarians to Bureaucrats.* New York: Fawcett.
Safir, Shane & Dugan, Jamila. (2021). *Street Data.* Thousand Oaks, CA: Corwin.
Sanders, George. (2000). *The Very Persistent Gappers of FRIP.* New York: Villard.
Sinek, Simon. (2009). *Start with Why.* New York: Penguin.
Sommers, William. (2021). *Creating Talent Density.* Lanham, MD: Rowman & Littlefield.
Surowiecki, James. (2004). *The Wisdom of Crowds.* New York: Anchor Books.
The True Story of a Grateful Whale. (n.d.). www.inspirationpeak.com. Retrieved April 24, 2024, from http://www.inspirationpeak.com/cgi-bin/stories.cgi?record=51#:~:text=Ifpercent20youpercent20readpercent20thepercent20front,topercent20strugglepercent20topercent20staypercent20afloat.
Walsh, David. (1994). *Selling Out America's Children.* Minneapolis: Fairview.
Wenger, Etienne. (1998). *Communities of Practice.* Cambridge, UK: Cambridge University Press.
Wheatley, Margaret. (2012). *Turning to One Another.* New York: Penguin.
Zander, Rosamund Stone & Zander, Benjamin. *The Art of Possibility.* Harvard Business School Press, 2000, pp. 52–53.

Chapter 4

Coaching

"Nothing happens without personal transformation."

—W. Edward Deming

WHY THIS TOPIC?

Essential Coaching Skills for Strong Leadership

Coaching provides support as individuals, teams, and organizations move toward positive transformation. Coaching is a reflective method used to develop increased performance to support thinking, problem solving, planning, and navigating change. Jon Gordon describes coaching as looking for ways to learn, apply, improve, and grow.

Outside of education, who has the most coaches? CEOs, leaders with high potential, professional athletes, and musicians all have coaches; some of them have more than one coach. People who want to improve seek coaching.

How do we make coaching a sought after process in education? We make coaching a clear process and remove the mystery or threat.

1. Communicate with our teams a clear definition of coaching. The International Coaching Federation defines coaching as partnering with clients in a thought-provoking and creative process that inspires them to maximize their personal and professional potential. The process of coaching often unlocks previously untapped sources of imagination, productivity, and leadership. Develop a clear definition of coaching in your organization that aligns with your values.

2. Make clear agreements about how coaching takes place, who receives coaching, and what is shared about the coaching interactions. Communicate

this information to the entire team. Provide clear pathways for people to request coaching.

3. Begin coaching leaders first. Make coaching a sought after commodity by first engaging team and campus leaders rather than coaching individuals in need of assistance. If we coach people on a path to a growth plan only, coaching becomes a process tainted by failure. Set up coaching for success and have everyone want a coach of their own.

The benefits of coaching are:

- improved performance
- employee retention
- motivation and movement beyond our comfort zones (Gordon, pp. 47–49)

Key lessons from *The Coaching Habit*:

1. Listen more than you speak
2. Additional questions for your toolbox
3. Make room for learning

Effective coaches empower the employees they coach to think deeply, explore options, develop their own plans, and draw their own conclusions. Coaches develop self-efficacy and higher level thinking through their others-centered communication skills: listening, paraphrasing, pausing, and asking powerful questions. Michael Bungay Stanier says advice is a monster. Advice creates distance between people and chokes higher level problem solving. Believe in the capacity of others to solve their own problems. Offer advice with caution and permission.

Additional questions for your toolbox:

- The foundation question: What do you want?
- The support question: What would most support your thinking?
- The data question: How is student data informing what you want to work on?
- The success question: What does success look like?
- The strategic question: If you are saying "yes" to this, what are you saying "no" to?

Remember to make room for learning. People do not automatically build a new habit or make use of new information. They need to be able to reflect on new knowledge so they can experience a "click" moment. To make room for learning, ask the learning question: What was most useful for you?

QUOTES TO START CONVERSATIONS

"A good coach can change a game. A great coach can change a life." —John R. Wooden

"With the right kind of coaching and determination you can accomplish anything." —Reese Witherspoon

"Coaching is one of the most effective leadership styles that can transform, empower, and unlock people's potential. Ask more, give advice less, and elevate your impact forever." —Farshad Asl

"Coaching offers a safe place to think, to reflect, to speak truthfully, to ask questions—about self and others." —*Results Coaching: The New Essential for School Leaders*, p. 13

"What goals would you be setting for yourself if you knew you could not fail?" —Robert H. Schuller

STORIES

People progress at different rates through the challenges of life and periods of growth. As a result, we need different mental models at different times in our lives. A well-timed story, metaphor, or proverb can shift our thinking and generate more productive actions. A seasoned leader sent this email to their staff with the subject:

Four Kinds of Power
By Sally Helgesen

Sally Helgesen in her blog introduced the concept of power by Ted Jenkins. Here is the blog:

Ted Jenkins was a senior engineer at Intel who had been with the company since its founding. When I was doing interviews at the company years ago for my book *The Web of Inclusion*, people kept telling me, "You have to talk to Ted."

I'm glad I did, because he gave me one of those lightbulb moments that forever shifted how I think about power.

When I asked Ted why Intel had a history of getting and using strategic ideas from people at every level, he said it was because the company recognized that four kinds of power always operate in organizations, and understood that being able to draw on all four kinds of power increases an organization's ability to innovate—and to create a cohesive culture.

The four kinds of power Ted laid out for me are:

- the power of position
- the power of expertise
- the power of personal authority
- the power of connections

Most of us are familiar with the power of position, which is determined by our title, our job description, and our place in the chain of command—where we stand on the official organization chart. But while positional power is substantial, giving us formal control over specific resources and the right to make certain decisions, it is always extrinsic, unrelated to our individual talents or merits. This means that however exalted, our position is always a slot that we are temporarily filling. It preexists our tenure and will endure after we have gone.

The power of expertise is embedded in the skills and knowledge we bring to our jobs and those we develop over time, through training, or by daily practice. Because these skills are lodged in our brains and wired into our bodies, they are intrinsic to us in a way that positional power never can be. Whether innate or learned, they are always self-renewing, increasing with use rather than diminishing. And we take this power with us if and when we leave the organization.

The power of connections is vested in our personal relationships. These include the one- to six-degrees-of-separation acquaintances we can call upon when needed. A robust web of such connections operating throughout a company enables resources, ideas, and information to flow anywhere they can be useful, creating opportunities for innovation. The power of connections is the reason that high-functioning teams can transform an entire organization; people know how to find skills in unexpected places.

The power of personal authority resides in our ability to inspire trust and respect among people we work with, regardless of the position we hold. Personal authority may be, and often is, wildly disproportionate to positional power: the supply chain clerk who helps identify a new distribution link, the admin who serves as a top executive's eyes and ears. Having strong personal authority often spurs colleagues to seek out our observations and judgments, which increases their power as well as ours.

Ted Jenkins also noted that, in toxic organizations, leaders tend to view the broad distribution of expertise, connections, and personal authority as a threat to their own positional power rather than a resource they can draw on to make the enterprise stronger. Their reluctance to nurture and honor other kinds of power results in widespread de-motivation and a diminished capacity for innovation and growth. Although these weaknesses may take time to become manifest, information and resource logjams are the most typical immediate consequences for organizations that over-privilege positional power.

Ted Jenkins was a man before his time, perhaps even before our time. His ideas are still revolutionary today.

Discussion Questions

- What kind of power do you most identify with?
- What kind of power does your coachee use most in their interactions?
- What is one positive action you might take to promote your own or others positive use of power in their organization?

Add your own questions/reflections:

1.
2.
3.
4.
5.

Coaching Versus Telling

Yolanda, an experienced leadership coach, learned a lesson. While coaching Tyronne, a new elementary principal, she found that telling, giving directions, and suggesting actions were not working as well. Yolanda found that telling robbed Tyronne of the learning developed by creating his own solutions, became more efficacious when putting his plan into action, and reduced the pressure to be right.

Another lesson Yolanda learned was that although the district prided itself in treating each school equally, that was not equity. Equity was a major initiative for the district. As well-meaning as the plan was, adapting to each school became more apparent. Tyronne was leading a STEM school, which had some differences in addition to a more diverse population.

STEM required different equipment, deeper professional development, and making sure the community knew the curriculum. Tyronne, being a first year principal, believed nothing was impossible and his energy was a model for the staff.

Tyronne continued to deal with the equality versus equity issue inside the district. The district remained firm and indicated that Tyronne would have to raise the money for a STEM lab.

Yolanda helped Tyronne focus on raising the money rather than the impossible task of getting funding from the district. Yolanda, the coach, refocused on plans for raising the $1 million to support STEM, the students, and the community.

When issues were raised, Yolanda responded with, "Say more about that," and "In what way can we move forward?" Taking a page from Michael Stainer Bungay, Yolanda would use the strategy AWE—and what else—to further specify the plan.

With the continual support of his coach Yolanda, Tyronne developed and presented to the PTO, made appearances at the local service organizations, and wrote articles in the newspaper. When the principal had about $400,000, he visited with the superintendent. The superintendent decided to match the $400,000, which was a major accomplishment. Finally, in the spring he called his coach, "We have our one million dollars." What a relief.

Yolanda recalls this was a great experience and lesson. What if I had given her advice? How would the outcome be different?

Discussion Questions

- How do you express belief in others? How do you tame your advice monster?
- What does it feel like when someone believes in you?
- Who needs you to believe in them?

Add your own questions/reflections:

1.
2.
3.
4.
5.

Bill and Lindsey were fortunate to spend time in a workshop led by Edgar Schein prior to his passing. His works have been foundational for many leaders, he has written many books on organizational development, and he was a master at asking questions getting to the heart of the matter.

Here are links to two summaries of books that Schein has written:

- https://learningomnivores.com/what-were-reading/humble-inquiry/
- https://learningomnivores.com/what-were-reading/helping/

Humble Inquiry
By Edgar Schein

One of the stories he used was about a leadership meeting he attended to provide feedback to the CEO. After meeting the CEO, Schein asked what could make the time together more useful. The CEO said, "We never get to very important issues."

Schein asked the CEO, "Who sets the agenda for the meeting?" The response was the executive secretary provides the agenda.

Schein asked the executive secretary to join the conversation. Schein asked how she determined the order of the issues. Her response was, "I just take them in order as people call in to add to the agenda." Schein said, "Thank you." She left.

Edgar then asked the CEO, "Could you prioritize the agenda prior to the meeting?" AHA.

Bill was called into shadow six high school principals by the associate superintendent in an urban district. The associate superintendent wanted to know if she could help principals spend more time on instruction rather than management. She wanted Bill to come and spend a half day with each principal.

Bill said, "I can tell you for free on this phone call." The associate superintendent said, "You have to come and see for yourself." (Bill has been a high school principal for 25 years.) Again, Bill offered his help for no cost. The associate superintendent insisted he get on a plane and come to the city. After three days shadowing six principals, he returned home. The associate superintendent called two days later to find out what he recommended.

Bill said, "I have a couple of questions":

B: When a parent calls you about a parking permit at the school, what do you do?

AS: I call the principal to solve the problem.

B: So, dealing with parking is a priority versus observing a math class.

B: You have meetings with the high school principals. How much time do you discuss instruction, collaboration, and leadership?

AS: It's always on the agenda.

54   Chapter 4

B: That is not what asked you. How much time do you spend discussing instruction and leadership issues?

AS: We never get to that.

B: So, you spend time with the "killer Bs"—buses, budgets, and boundaries.

B: If instruction and leadership are not more important than parking permits and not discussed when you have meetings as a priority, why would you think the principals would interpret it is a priority?

The point being, you have to model and reward the behavior you want instead of signaling time spent is the priority issue. (Based on a true exchange between Bill and an associate superintendent.)

Here are some of Edgar Schein's questions that will be helpful:

Problem-Focused Humble Inquiry

- Tell me about what you have in mind?
- Why do you want to do . . . ?
- What problem are you trying to solve?
- How is what we are doing really helping?

ACTIVITY

Know what the other person really needs to know before jumping in and providing answers:

- Assess your ignorance and allow curiosity to lead the conversation.
- Ask for examples to clarify general statements and push thinking.
- Listen intently and frame questions from a stance of curiosity.
- Stay open to questions, no one question is ever the right question.

What questions do you use to identify processes and procedures that restrict action or reduce the response gaps in meetings?

See table 4.1 for a few examples of traps and humble inquiry.

Table 4.1. Comparison Questions.

Confrontational Question	Relationship Trap	Humble Inquiry	Elicits
"Did that make you angry?"	Projecting values on others	"How did that make you feel?"	Feelings and reactions
"Do you think they sat that way because they were scared?"	Having a priori or fixed expectations	"Why do you suppose they sat that way?"	Causes and motives
"Why didn't you say something to the group?"	Meeting defensiveness with more pressure	"What did you do?"	Actions
"Were the others in the room surprised?"	Projecting values on others	"How did the others react?"	Shared systems and situations

Discussion Questions

- How do these questions challenge your thinking about coaching?
- What are the key moments that make you a better educator?
- What is one thing you can do to promote learning moments for others?

Add your own questions/reflections:

1.
2.
3.
4.
5.

There are many coaching models and philosophies being taught in organizations. Some are behavioral, some are cognitive, sales coaching, life coaching, and the list goes on. What is common to multiple models is promoting a growth mindset and positive individual or organizational change. Coaching has become one of the fastest growing industries in the world. What is common to coaching initiatives is promoting healthy change within an organization. The goal of this book is to set the stage for whatever the organization has decided to promote.

Discussion Questions

- What helps you make a change?
- What is a time that you made a shift or change that produced a great outcome?
- How can you raise your own awareness about areas in your life that you want to change?

Add your own questions/reflections:

1.
2.
3.
4.
5.

VIDEOS

Mo Cheeks Helps Girl With National Anthem (2:10 minutes)

https://www.youtube.com/watch?v=q4880PJnO2E

There are many times in life and our profession that we need support without judgment. This video demonstrates that sometimes, when you least expect it and need help, those with courage to step up are the heroes and she-roes in life.

An eighth grade student chosen to sing the national anthem at a professional basketball game forgets the lyrics. See Mo Cheeks, the coach of the Philadelphia 76ers, step in and step up to support her. His example of side-by-side coaching is inspirational. This is what we want for adults and children.

Discussion Questions

- What is an example of a time that someone offered you support as you faced a challenge?
- What supports you most when you are facing fear?
- What resources do you have to help you overcome challenges?

Add your own questions/reflections:

1.
2.

3.
4.
5.

J-MAC (2:15 minutes)

https://www.bing.com/videos/riverview/relatedvideo?q=J-MAC+hoops+dreams&mid=DEDE465F9F53D703789BDEDE465F9F53D703789B&FORM=VIRE

School coaches and advisors have a special relationship with students. They focus on bringing the best out of the students, team, school, and community. The best coaches/advisors and schools embrace diversity, engage all students, and model what a caring community does.

Discussion Questions

- Have you ever had a fatal flaw that got in your way of success?
- What helped you deal with the flaw and change the flaw into a positive context?
- Who are your models for overcoming a difficult attribute?

Add your own questions/reflections:

1.
2.
3.
4.
5.

Volkswagen Ski Mask Commercial (1:02 minutes)

https://youtu.be/6wzxg2Goz3I?feature=sharedpresumingpositiveintent

> "Coaching aligns with what years and decades of research continues to support: that as human beings we do our best, think our best, and work our best when others believe in our best."
>
> —*Results Coaching: The New Essential for School Leaders*

Discussion Questions

- How do you practice assuming the best of others?
- What are some ways to practice looking for the best in others?
- What are the repercussions of viewing others with a negative lens?

Add your own questions/reflections:

1.
2.
3.
4.
5.

QUOTES TO PROMOTE COACHING

"A good coach will make his players see what they can be rather than what they are." —Ara Parasheghian

"You get the best effort from others not by lighting a fire beneath them, but by building a fire within." —Bob Nelson

"Coaching is unlocking a person's potential to maximize their growth." —John Whitmore

"Everything in coaching hinges on listening because what we are listening for affects where we are speaking from and unfolds how we are being with and for each other." —Marilyn Atkinson and Rae Chois

"Good coaching is good teaching and nothing else." —Pat Conroy

"Leadership is the ability to guide others without force into a direction or decision that leaves them still feeling empowered and accomplished." —Lisa Cash Hanson

"To lead people, walk behind them." —Lao Tzu

"I believe that wherever there is mastery, coaching is occurring and whenever coaching is done, mastery will be the outcome." —Andrea J. Lee

"The best coaches really care about people. They have a sincere interest in people." —Byron and Catherine Pulsifer

"Our conversations invent us. Through our speech and our silence, we become smaller or larger selves, we diminish or enhance the other person, and we narrow or expand the possibilities between us. How we use our voice determines the quality of our relationships, who we are in the world, and what the world can be and might become. Clearly, a lot is at stake here." —Harriet Lerner, *The Dance of Connection*

EXTENSION ACTIVITY

Sell It To Me

Sell It To Me is an improv activity that can be done in pairs. It provides opportunities for participants to practice their persuasion. Follow these steps to engage your team:

- Each participant has 10–15 seconds to grab a nearby object.
- Have participants pair up and bring the object they selected.
- Take turns of approximately 1 minute to make a convincing sales pitch to sell the item to the partner.
- Partners can nominate a participant to share their sales pitch with the group.

Debriefing Questions

- How does it feel to be on the receiving end of the sales pitch?
- What motivates you to buy into an idea or change?
- What is the difference between coaching and a sales pitch?

As leaders, we need multiple conversational strategies because of different situations, different people, and different outcomes. Figure 4.1 identifies nine such conversational strategies from the left side (most reflective, coach-like) to the right side (most restrictive, directive).

- Which strategy do you need to have with a direct report or supervisor?
- Which strategy do you respond best to for being the most productive?
- How do you practice these skills based on the context of the situation?
- Using figure 4.1, how many of the conversational strategies do you feel comfortable with using?
- What is one area for you or your team to focus on to get even better results?

SUMMARY QUESTIONS

- How do the stories and/or videos help you "make the case" for coaching?
- What other learnings can be gleaned from these stories/videos?
- How do these stories/videos connect to your organization's values?

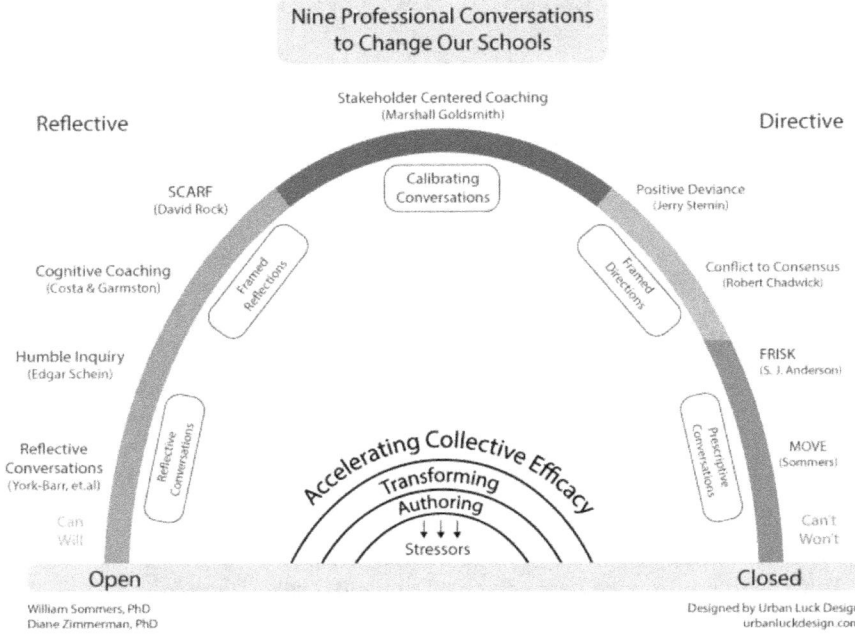

Figure 4.1. Nine Professional Conversations. *William Sommers.*

BIBLIOGRAPHY

Bambrick-Santoyo, Paul. (2012). *Leverage Leadership.* San Francisco: Jossey-Bass.
Block, Peter. (2002). *The Answer to How Is Yes.* San Francisco: Berrett-Koehler.
Erikson, Thomas. (2021). *Surrounded by Bad Bosses (and Lazy Employees): How to Stop Struggling, Start Succeeding, and Deal with Idiots at Work.* New York: St. Martin's.
Goldsmith, Marshall. (2007). *What Got You Here Won't Get You There.* New York: Hyperion.
Grant, Adam. (2013). *Give and Take.* New York: Viking.
Helgesen, Sally & Goldsmith, Marshall. (2018). *How Women Rise.* New York: Hachette Books.
Helgesen, Sally. (2023). *Rising Together: How We Can Bridge Divides and Create a More Inclusive Workplace.* New York: Hachette.
Schein, Edgar. (2009). *Helping: How to Offer, Give, and Receive Help.* San Francisco: Berrett-Koehler Publishers, Inc.
Schein, Edgar. (2013). *Humble Inquiry: The Gentle Art of Asking Instead of Telling.* San Francisco: Berrett-Koehler.
Scott, Kim. (2017). *Radical Candor.* New York: St. Martin's Press.

Sommers, William & Zimmerman, Diane. (2018). *9 Conversations to Change Schools.* Thousand Oaks, CA: Corwin Press.
Stanier, Michael Bungay. (2016). *The Coaching Habit: Say Less, Ask More & Change the Way You Lead Forever.* Ontario, CA: Box of Crayons Press.
Wiseman, Liz. (2021). *The Impact Players.* New York: Harper Collins.

Chapter 5

Change

"Life is change, growth is optional. Choose wisely."

—Karen Kaiser Clark

WHY THIS TOPIC?

Technology, more countries entering the economic environment, innovation, and so on are driving change. Does anyone believe this will end any time soon? Our children and students will live in a different world than the one the adults grew up in.

Neil Postman said, "Children are messages to a world we will not see." Buying food, supplies, clothes, and so on has been a challenge for people who grew up talking to a checkout clerk, building a relationship with the post office staff, and knowing the folks at our corner gas station and employees at other establishments as friends.

From the book by Marshall Goldsmith (2007) *What Got You Here Won't Get You There: The Success Delusion, or Why We Resist Change*: "You probably feel like the bear, we'd like to suggest you're the salmon."

This was an ad from an insurance company. It is a powerful ad. We in the workplace delude ourselves about our achievements, our status, and our contributions. Goldsmith's research found that leaders had the following tendencies:

- They overestimate their contribution to a project.
- They take credit, partial or complete, for successes that truly belongs to others.
- They have an elevated opinion of their professional skills and standing (ranking higher) among their peers.

- They conveniently ignore the costly failures and time-consuming dead ends they created.
- They exaggerate their projects' impact on the net profits (outcomes) because they discount the real and hidden costs built in.

All of these delusions are direct results of success, not failure. People get positive reinforcement from past successes. However, it erases doubt and can lead to inflated perceptions of self. It can blind leaders to the risks and challenges in their work. Some people say that if leaders had a complete grip on reality, seeing every situation for exactly what it is, they wouldn't get out of bed in the morning! Leadership is hard work and can be overwhelming. Our (mild) delusions can give us hope and keep us going but our delusions become a serious liability when we need to change and are unwilling or unaware of the need.

Here are three potential parts of a leader's perceptions that may indicate there's a problem:

1. We think the other party is confused.
2. It dawns on us that maybe the other party is not confused, maybe their information about our perceived shortcomings is inaccurate—we have to justify the confusion as we are still in denial mode.
3. When all else fails, we attack the other party!

Those are possible initial surface responses—the denial mechanisms. Couple them with the very positive interpretations that successful people assign to:

- their past performance
- their ability to influence their success
- their optimistic belief that their success will continue in the future
- their sense of control over their own destiny

and you may have a recipe for disaster! The paradox of success: these beliefs that carried us here may be holding us back in our quest to go there. The following stories and videos can help focus people on the process of change and how to contend with a changing world.

QUOTES TO PROMOTE CHANGE

"You can fight change, adapt to change, embrace change, create change, and/or lead change. No matter your choice, it's not going away." —George Couros

"If you don't like change, you will like irrelevance a lot less." —General Erik Shinseki

"Nature has a funny way of breaking what does not bend." —Alice Walker

"Never doubt that a small group of thoughtful, committed individuals can change the world. In fact, it's the only thing that ever has." —Margret Mead

"Every great dream begins with a dreamer. Always remember, you have within you the strength, the patience, and the passion to reach for the stars to change the world." —Harriet Tubman

STORIES

The following story might help those with experience to build systems to reduce risk and make it safe for those who follow.

"Show Them a Way"
By Bill Sommers

"If I have seen further [than others], it is by standing on the shoulders of giants."
—1675 letter by Isaac Newton

Who are your giants? What models of behavior do you have? Who or where did you get that knowledge and skills. As productive adults, we have all benefitted from those who gave us their time and attention to teach us. Mostly through modeling, personal instruction, and even more from coaching us to excel.

Indigenous cultures always revered the elders, for they had more knowledge and experience. Positive cultures depend on passing on thoughts, behaviors, and attitudes to teach our children.

So the question is, are you building bridges to the future for those who will follow you? We have all benefitted from parents, teachers, coaches, and advisors along our path to growth. There will be many who follow us as we have followed others. If the path has been cleared of barriers, potholes, and detours, those who follow will reach a better place because of what we have left behind from our efforts.

Those who follow us can be aided by our trial and errors, new knowledge created, and acting in community.

> "Communities are built from the assets and gifts of their citizens, not from the citizens' needs or deficiencies. Sustainable transformation is constructed in those places where citizens choose to come together to produce a desired future."
>
> —Peter Block (2009)

Community: The Structure of Belonging

So, how might you contribute to the community to leave a legacy for those who follow our path? Will you make it easier to advance and provide to unleash talent by removing and reducing barriers?

Ego strength is important for leaders. Ego can be the enemy of good decision making. My late friend Chris Coffey once told me, "Too much ego, amigo." That has stuck with me.

Ego can make us continue to move forward when the results are not working. Setting aside ego and thinking about the next iteration of a procedure or group who will pass can help leaders make the changes that build the bridges and close the gaps.

Discussion Questions

- What do you think were some of the leadership traits the elder possessed that are beneficial to an organization?
- What were the reflective thoughts that can change our focus and attitude?
- What could the fellow pilgrim, as the leader, learn from the old man?

Add your own questions/reflections:

1.
2.
3.
4.
5.

In the book *Communities of Practice*, Etienne Wenger answers the question, "How do people learn the ways of the organization?" Yes, most organizations have policy manuals. Our litigious system requires written policies. At the same time, rarely does the policy manual answer every question.

An example might be a limit of sick leave, a highly effective teacher, and a dying parent. Life changes require humanity at times. Some of the issues the authors have had to confront are not in the policy manual. (*Note*: you can't write the stuff we have had to deal with.)

Wenger posits that people watch how the organization operates rather than referring to the manual. Instead of looking at the manual, most employees ask their colleagues on how to do things. The transfer of knowledge and skills is extremely important in making the organization responsive to the stakeholders/customers/clients (students, parents, and staff).

Discussion Questions

- What are some of the responsive behaviors within our organization?
- What were the reflective thoughts that can support organizational change?
- What could the leader do to encourage the transfer of knowledge and skills in order to support change?

Add your own questions/reflections:

1.
2.
3.
4.
5.

The following story has been widely distributed on the internet. In a Google search, a story of the *Five Monkeys* appeared. We don't know which came first. However, this story has been used in many workshops to illustrate the power of change or lack thereof.

Gorilla Story

This story starts with a cage containing five gorillas and a large bunch of bananas hanging above some stairs in the center of the cage. Before long, a gorilla will go to the stairs and start to climb toward the bananas. As soon as he touches the stairs, all of the gorillas are sprayed with cold water.

After a while another gorilla will make an attempt with the same result—all are sprayed with cold water. Every time a gorilla attempts to retrieve the bananas, they are sprayed with cold water until they quit trying and leave the bananas alone.

One of the original five gorillas is removed from the cage and replaced with a new one. The new gorilla sees the bananas and starts to climb the stairs. To his horror, all the other gorillas attack him. After another attempt and attack, he knows that if he tries to climb the stairs, he will be assaulted.

Next, the second of the original five gorillas is replaced with a new one. The newcomer goes to the stairs and is attacked. The previous newcomer takes part in the punishment with enthusiasm.

Next, the third original gorilla is replaced with a new one. The new one makes it to the stairs and is attacked as well. Two of the four gorillas that beat him have no idea why they were not permitted to climb the stairs or why they are participating in the beating of the newest gorilla.

After the fourth and fifth original gorillas have been replaced, all the gorillas, which were sprayed with cold water, are gone. Nevertheless, no gorilla will ever again approach the stairs. Why not?

An explanation of the original study that examined primate behavior can be found in the article "It Is Just the Way We Do Things Around Here" (https://www.harapnuik.org/?p=3158).

> "Because that's the way it's always been done."
> —Author unknown, based on a widely circulated email

Discussion Questions

- What could one of the original gorillas do to change the outcome?
- What could a new gorilla do to change the outcome?
- How is your organization like the gorilla story?
- What can you do to change the outcome?

Add your own questions/reflections:

1.
2.
3.
4.
5.

In many classrooms, experienced teachers are saying students have changed. Every generation changes based on new research, emotional markers of history, and changing family structures. To address this, Michael Grinder teaches about dogs and cats.

Dogs are loyal, love attention, and normally fall in line with expectations. Cats, however, are independent, self-selective, and not prone to take immediate direction. We don't imply that students are animals but the metaphor may offer some new ideas.

Many teachers were taught and came into education teaching dogs. Students who perform like cats are increasing in numbers. Hence, how do we teach more cats than dogs in our classrooms?

There Are CATS in Our DOG HOUSE
Inspired by Michael Grinder and the story *When Children Turn into Cats* by Lara Adair

If you have worked in schools or have had children many years ago, see if you can relate to this story. In the schools, children of all ages attended schools designed from an industrial model, went to classes when the bell rang, sat up straight, and the teacher told them what they needed to know. Schools, books, and encyclopedias were the main source of information.

Most homes had a breadwinner who determined when meals were served, what chores needed to be done, and most children complied with requests by their parents or teachers.

Children are not animals, but consider this metaphor. Children were more doglike. Dogs tend to follow directions of the owner, crave positive attention, respond to shame and reprimands, and desperately want approval from the person in charge.

Cats, on the other hand, respond differently. Cats are more independent. Give them an order and they look at you and think, "Who do you think you are?" Cats do what they want and when they want in order to do something. They play with anything that gets their attention. If they make a mistake, they internally say, "That's what I meant to do. So what? Don't judge me!"

As a longtime educator and parent, it dawned on me, as Michael Grinder used this metaphor in a workshop, I was taught to teach and lead dogs (students and staff). Coming out of retirement several times it seemed like I was leading cats (students and staff). It seems the percentage of cats continues to multiply at a fast pace, while the structure in schools and families were still thinking they were leading dogs. There are more cats in the dog house (schools and homes) than dogs.

As young children, they are dependent upon their parents and teachers. As they become older, some start exhibiting cat behavior. The little girls and boys who used to look to adults for positive reinforcement are now looking at their peers, media, and society for models. As they end the elementary schools years and enter middle school, cats blossom. Some no longer take direction easily or are as compliant. Remember, we are raising our kids to be self-reliant, creative, and find their own pathway. And they are. Doggone it. Doglike behavior is gone or reduced.

When they do, most of us want them to continue to be doglike and in the adolescent years they are more catlike. Frustration sets in, oppositional defiant disorder (ODD) abounds, and control is harder to maintain. In the final analysis we want our children safe and *yes*, it can be a struggle.

Be patient. Most times dog behavior will return, just not on your timetable. As our kids move from high school there is still experimentation for a time. If you have younger children, you are asking yourself, "Yah, when?" It is never soon enough when you are the parent or the educator.

Most of the time, as the young person matures, they understand more fully what their parents or educators were trying their best to do. At some point, usually in mid-twenties or later, more doglike behavior returns from the wild times in school and post-high school. As they get older, they sometimes even ask for your opinion, advice, or experience, especially when they have their own children.

So, if you are struggling with your own cats and their behavior, there will be a time when the doglike behavior returns. I guarantee it won't be soon enough. It will be on the time schedule of cats. Even cats want acceptance, love, and to know they are valued.

As a school principal for many years, staff or individual adults still might be in their cat phase. Focus on the primary goal of getting young people ready for life after high school. That is where they will spend the majority of their time.

Discussion Questions

- What are teaching strategies that attract the curiosity of catlike students?
- How can you use the creativity of catlike students with the more moderate behavior of doglike students?
- How do you build a classroom to accommodate both types of students?

Add your own questions/reflections:

1.
2.
3.
4.
5.

VIDEOS

Be Open-Minded (1:02 minutes)

https://www.bing.com/videos/search?q=PBS+video%2c+skunk&docid=603552688789523800&mid=4933D06261D9378662A44933D06261D9378662A4&view=detail&FORM=VIRE

You know when you have a belief in your mind and it is hard to see any other possibilities? There are times when one picture, one new piece of information, or a person with a new idea can change our perception. Many in history made us think differently. Johan Kepler, Albert Einstein, and Steve Jobs are examples of those who changed life as we know it. This video is a short but impactful way to change perception in one moment.

Discussion Questions

- What are some of the assumptions I hold about myself and others?
- What are some of the things that I can do to be more resilient in the face of change?
- What are some of the beliefs that I have that might be limiting me?

Add your own questions/reflections:

1.
2.
3.
4.
5.

Be More Aura (1 minute)

https://www.youtube.com/watch?v=W6U4FCSaSIc

This video shows how change starts small and spreads. A smile can start a chain of positive energy that spreads across a room or even across your campus! Some teachers stand at the door of their classroom with a positive greeting each day to start off with a positive interaction. You may have encountered people who make you nervous while others relax you. How do we share positive energy with others? Consider this as you watch the video.

Discussion Questions

- What kind of energy have you experienced when interacting with others?
- What examples of positive energy can you think of?
- What are small things you do to impact others?
- How can a leader's energy impact an organization?

Add your own questions/reflections:

1.
2.
3.

4.
5.

Boundin (4:41 minutes)

https://www.youtube.com/watch?v=CbDxtKx9FhE

One of the important jobs of leaders is to create and sustain hope, especially during times of change. The demands far exceed the staffing and financial resources to deal with all of the problems in education. Schools need wrap-around services for students, especially in low SES communities.

This video by Pixar provides a few strategies to change the "mope" to "hope."

Discussion Questions

- Change will continue. The only question is, how will we deal with change? Lynch and Kordis have a quote: "It's not what happens to you, it is how you respond to what happens to you that determines the experience."
- How do you deal with change?
- How do you incorporate change and what has worked in the past?

Add your own questions/reflections:

1.
2.
3.
4.
5.

QUOTES TO PROMOTE CHANGE

"Knowing what must be done does away with fear." —Rosa Parks

"You can make things happen. You're in control of change." —Dyllan McGee

"I believe in change. I believe in the power it has to unite us and ignite us." —Uzo Aduba

"Education is the most powerful weapon which you can use to change the world." —Nelson Mandela

"The secret of change is to focus all of your energy not on fighting the old but on building the new." —Socrates

"If you can't fly, then run. If you can't run, then walk. If you can't walk, then crawl. But whatever you do, you have to keep moving forward." —Martin Luther King Jr.

"Change will not come if we wait for some other person or some other time. We are the ones we've been wishing for. We are the change that we seek." —Barack Obama

"Change is the end result of all true learning." —Leo F. Buscaglia

"What *people* resist is not *change* per se but *loss*." —Ronald Heifetz

"Change: Rocks, rivers, or wet babies." —Bill Sommers

EXTENSION ACTIVITY

Switch Places

The Switch Places exercise is a simple but powerful change management activity. This exercise helps team members to understand each other's point of view and different perspectives. The hidden lesson of this exercise is to manage resistance to change by knowing and understanding perspectives of others.

This change management activity motivates your team members to step outside of their comfort zones and consider alternative viewpoints.

How to do this activity:
1. Create a circle of chairs and put an object in the center.
2. Once the employees are seated, ask them to look at the object and explain that object.
3. Ask them to stand up and switch seats after a while.
4. Invite them again to explain the object from their changed position.

Force-Field Analysis

One particular change you want to see or investigate should be written on a huge poster or board. Label the left column "driving forces" and the right column "restraining forces" on your board by drawing a line along the center. Consider what motivating factors will advance the transformation and what inhibiting factors will work against it.

Write a rating of 0 to 5 next to each force to indicate whether or not it will have a beneficial or detrimental effect on the change. Think of ways to strengthen the group's identified driving factors and weaken its restraining ones.

This exercise's major goal is to balance these forces such that your driving forces are more potent than your restraining forces.

Cross Your Arms

Instruct the participants to cross their arms wherever they feel most at ease. Once they are relaxed, ask them to fold their arms the opposite way. Ask them what they feel as long as they maintain their arms crossed.

The major goal of this activity is to make them realize that transition can first be uneasy and difficult and how change does not always feel comfortable. But if change is sustained for a certain time, it becomes natural and comfortable.

Musical Tunes for Change

A fun way to introduce change to a team is with music. Pick a few of the tunes below and play a few sound clips. Have the team name that tune and/or determine what the songs have in common.

Songs for name that tune:

- "Man in the Mirror"—Michael Jackson
- "A Change Would Do You Good"—Sheryl Crow
- "Waiting on the World to Change"—John Mayer
- "The Change"—Garth Brooks
- "Change"—Taylor Swift
- "Change the World"—Eric Clapton
- "That's How You Change the World"—Newsboys
- "Change"—Carrie Underwood

SUMMARY QUESTIONS

- How do the stories and/or videos help you "make the case" for change?
- What other learnings can be gleaned from these stories/videos?
- How do these stories/videos connect to your organization's values?

BIBLIOGRAPHY

Abrahamson, Eric. (2004). *Change without Pain.* Boston: Harvard Business Press.

Banaji, Mahzarin & Greenwald, Anthony. (2013). *Blind Spot: The Hidden Biases of Good People.* New York: Random House.

Bridges, William. (1991). *Managing Transitions: Making the Most of Change.* New York: Addison-Wesley Publishing Company, Inc.

Deutschman, Alan. (2007). *Change or Die.* New York: HarperCollins.

Gordon, J. (2009). *The Shark and the Goldfish: Positive Ways to Thrive during Waves of Change.* Hoboken: John Wiley & Sons.

Grenny, J. et al. (2013). *Influencer: The New Science of Leading Change.* New York: VitalSmarts.

Kordis, Paul & Lynch, Dudley. (1988). *Strategy of the Dolphin.* New York: Fawcett-Columbine Book.

Kotter, John & Cohen, D. (2002). *The Heart of Change.* Boston: John P. Kotter and Deloitte Consulting LLC.

Payne, Charles. (2008). *So Much Reform, So Little Change.* Cambridge: Harvard Education Press.

Seagal, S. & Horne, D. (1997). *Human Dynamics.* Waltham, MA: Pegasus Communications.

Chapter 6

Conflict

"The trouble with the rat race is that even when you win, you're still a rat."

—Jane Wagner

WHY THIS TOPIC?

Conflict is not always negative. *Cognitive Conflict* (Amason et al.) defines the difference between cognitive and affective conflict. Cognitive dissonance can produce better solutions. It is not personal. Affective responses can be emotional and may at times tear collaboration apart.

In the leadership class we teach at the university level, we often start with the question, "How do you feel about dealing with conflict?" As students begin to squirm in their seats, we clarify: "We didn't ask you if you like it, we asked, 'How do you feel about dealing with conflict?'" We suggest if you really don't like dealing with conflict, school leadership may not be for you. Conflict abounds.

Peter Block in *Empowered Management* says there are five outcomes in a conflict:

- win/lose
- lose/win
- lose/lose
- win/win
- *no deal*

We suggest that if the negotiation is not win/win, no deal is the best option. The other three have at least one loser which causes negative consequences. Of course, we don't mean physical or psychological safety issues.

"Would you rather be right or happy?"

—Jerry Jampolsky

QUOTES TO START CONVERSATIONS

"I never lose. I either win or learn." —Nelson Mandela

"Relationships mean expectations and expectations can mean conflict." —Fred Knauer

"I have a self-made quote: Celebrate diversity, practice acceptance, and may we all choose peaceful options to conflict." —Donzella Michele Malone

"When you have a conflict, that means that there are truths that have to be addressed on each side of the conflict. And when you have a conflict, then it's an educational process to try to resolve the conflict. And to resolve that, you have to get people on both sides of the conflict involved so that they can dialogue." —Dolores Huerta

"An eye for an eye will only make the whole world blind." —Mahatma Gandhi

STORIES

Generations can occasionally come into conflict. The future can be unknown and scary. The past can be known and scary. Some things we don't want to repeat. However, we live in the present.

An experienced person can remember some of the things that worked and didn't work. A less experienced person might have some great ideas but not know how to minimize the unintended consequences.

The 10th Step
By Bill Sommers

We all make mistakes. The tenth step in Alcoholics Anonymous states, "When wrong, promptly admit it." The following story is about not promptly admitting it and a process to taking a step toward accepting responsibility.

A boss makes an attribution error. He assigns blame to his administrative assistant so he maintains apparent positional power. The real issue always comes out. Rumors quickly spread that he messed up, blamed his support staff, and publicly assigned blame.

The result, nobody trusts the leader because everyone soon knew he was the reason an error occurred and cost money, emotional stress, and the feeling each one of the coworkers might get the blame next time.

When we do make an error in judgment, offend a person, or have an ethical breakdown, we suggest the AAA model:

- *Accept* the responsibility of our actions.
- *Apologize* or make amends to the person harmed.
- Take *Action* to correct the inappropriate behavior.

People trust others who don't blame others, take responsibility for their part, and make amends. The correct thing to do is to take action to right the wrong. Stop ruminating, do something positive.

Discussion Questions

- What are some past relationships that may need repair?
- What is preventing you from making the necessary AAA steps?
- What is one thing you can do to correct past errors?

Add your own questions/reflections:

1.
2.
3.
4.
5.

The Power of the Badge
By Bill Sommers

A DEA officer stops at a ranch in Montana and talks with an old rancher. He tells the rancher, "I need to inspect your ranch for illegally grown drugs."

The old rancher says, "Okay, but do not go in that field over there" as he points out the location.

The DEA officer verbally explodes saying, "Mister, I have the authority of the federal government with me." Reaching into his rear pants pocket, he removes his badge and proudly displays it to the farmer. "See this badge? This badge means I am allowed to go wherever I wish . . . on any land. No questions asked or answers given. Have I made myself clear? Do you understand?" The old rancher nods politely, apologizes, and goes about his chores.

A short time later, the old rancher hears loud screams and sees the DEA officer running for his life, chased close behind by the rancher's prize bull. With every step the bull is gaining ground on the officer, and it seems likely that he'll get "horned" before he reaches safety. The officer is clearly terrified. The old rancher throws down his tools, runs to the fence, and yells at the top of his lungs: *Your badge . . . Show him your badge!*

Discussion Questions

- When has ego overtaken good thinking?
- What helps you when you are enmeshed in a solution/strategy/intervention that is not working as planned?
- Who do you go to when you need help?

Depends on Your Perspective
Told by Bob Chadwick

Bill spent 3 years before Bob passed learning consensus and conflict management from Bob. Bob was a forester specializing in bringing people together toward common understandings and actions to move forward from differing points of view.

This story is one Bob used to start the training with business, non profits, and education.

As the group formed in a room or in a large open space, he would stand in the middle and ask, "What do you see?"

First Perspective: Some of you see a screen for an LCD projector, chart paper, and an easel. You also see a wall with some posters.

Second Perspective: Some of you see several large windows, shades, and curtains.

Third Perspective: Some of you see two water fountains, two sets of doors, and garbage cans.

Fourth Perspective: And last, some of you see two hallways, stairs to the second floor, and the food service area.

What you believe is mostly what you see. Your view might interfere with other perspectives since you see the world one way and others see the world in another way. When we hunker down and refuse to ask questions about someone else's perspective, it is easy to get dug in to one view.

Bob then would continue with the process to manage unresolved conflict. Here is the process that many of us trained by Bob would use with two people, small groups, and with large groups.

When Bill became principal of a high school, there were inconsistencies in the adherence to what the student/parent handbook said. Some teachers let students wear hats, listen to headphones, and bring food into the classroom. Each of those were not allowed by the formal school rules. By late fall, lots of anger and discouragement were apparent.

There were about 125 certified staff, another 5 hall monitors, and 10 clerical positions. We took a staff development day and put everyone in a circle in the cafeteria. The goal was to get clear about what we will enforce and determine what we would change.

Step One: Line up by number of years of experience at the high school. (not necessarily years in education). Number off 1–14. All the 1's formed a group, all the 2's formed a group, and so on. The groups now had diversity of number of years at the school, each with a different perspective.

Step Two: Choose a facilitator and a recorder. We used chart paper and some groups more recently have used computers. Words are recorded exactly with the person's words, not translated by a recorder.

Step Three: Go around the group in order. No one has to speak *and* everyone has a chance to speak.

Step Four: Gain comments from each person. Changing facilitators and recorders for each question.

Question One: What are the issues for the staff to resolve? Facilitator makes sure everyone has a chance to speak, recorder transcribes the person's words.

Question Two: What is the worst possible outcome if we cannot gain consensus about how the school will operate?

Question Three: What is the best possible outcome if we can gain consensus about how the school will operate? *This is the goal or vision.*

Question Four: What strategies and actions are you willing to take to make the best possible outcome a reality? *These are action steps.*

Question Five: What will be the evidence that we are making progress toward the best possible outcome? *This is the assessment plan.*

Question Six: When will we meet again or how will the results be disseminated to the staff?

Step Five: Collate all responses and disseminate to staff so there is total transparency. A member from each team will meet to create themes for each question. The action steps identified by the most teams get put into place.

Step Six: Report on a regular basis of agreements made.

> "In essentials, we need unity.
> In non-essentials, we need flexibility.
> In everything, we need civility."
>
> —St. Augustine

Discussion Questions

- Have you ever encountered a time when someone or group behavior became a problem which had far reaching consequences? What did you do? What else could you have done?
- What questions or actions could you have taken to diffuse the situation?
- What is one thing you can do the next time?

Add your own questions/reflections:

1.
2.
3.
4.
5.

VIDEOS

Gazelle (37 seconds)

https://www.youtube.com/watch?v=LHuOzb9ezjY

Sometimes persistence and force pay off. Not all the time. You might become dinner for someone else. Instead of focusing only straight ahead, look around at the surroundings. There may be another way!

Discussion Questions

- Have you ever encountered a time when someone's skill became their detriment?
- What is the difference between the lion and the gazelle in terms of their motivation?
- What is the moral of the story between the lion and the gazelle?

Add your own questions/reflections:

1.
2.
3.
4.
5.

Many times conflict results from making judgements about the intentions of the other person. The commercials give several examples of making an assumption about the actions of another. We have used this as a conversation starter to identify when we have made the wrong assumption when the other person had the best of intentions.

Don't Judge Too Quickly (4:23 minutes)

https://www.youtube.com/watch?v=g_om7oc5EBE

We know that evolution has provided us with the skill of making assessments about potential threats—situations, people, and environments—that provide us with an advantage. Researchers tell us these assessments take about 10 seconds—we need that quickness to be able to fight, freeze, or flee! In nature, this author wouldn't have a chance trying to outrun most creatures in their habitat, save perhaps a sloth. While this ability is great for survival, it may not serve me well in our modern world where nuanced elements and interactions may need additional inference and interpretation! These clips are not only hilarious, they remind us that assuming may lead to making fundamental errors of judgment.

Discussion Questions

- Have you ever made the mistake of assuming you knew what was happening? The cause of the actions? The motivation of the other person?
- What strategies can you use to give a little space/time to consider all the options driving the behavior?

- What questions can I ask to be sure I have all the information I need to make a decision?

Add your own questions/reflections:

1.
2.
3.
4.
5.

Conflict with Friends (3:48 minutes)

https://www.youtube.com/watch?v=f_9eH8Ox-eU

The video demonstrates how two friends resolve conflict. Friends are eager to explain their point of view and provide unreasonable ultimatums which escalates the conflict.

Discussion Questions

- Have you ever made the mistake of assuming you knew what was happening? The cause of the actions? The motivation of the other person?
- What strategies can you use to give a little space to consider all the options driving the behavior?
- Who is a great model for demonstrating the ability to respond in a more timely matter than to jump to conclusions?

Add your own questions/reflections:

1.
2.
3.
4.
5.

Garbage Trucks (1:36 minutes)

https://www.youtube.com/watch?v=H4NW-Cqh308

Those without self control will cause more physical and emotional pain to themselves and others. See how a cab driver responds to an irate driver and teaches the rider a lesson.

Discussion Questions

- How do you respond when you receive a verbal attack?
- What strategies do you have to respond?
- What strategies would you like to add to your repertoire?

Add your own questions/reflections:

1.
2.
3.
4.
5.

QUOTES TO LEVERAGE CONFLICT

"What people often mean by getting rid of conflict is getting rid of diversity, and it is of utmost importance that these should not be considered the same. We may wish to abolish conflict, but we cannot get rid of diversity. Fear of difference is fear of life itself." —Mary Parker Follett

"Peace is not the absence of conflict but the ability to cope with it." —Mahatma Gandhi

"Conflict is the beginning of consciousness." —M. Esther Harding

"Change means movement. Movement means friction. Only in the frictionless vacuum of a nonexistent abstract world can movement or change occur without that abrasive friction of conflict." —Saul Alinsky

"If you talk to a man in a language he understands, that goes to his head. If you talk to him in his language, that goes to his heart." —Nelson Mandela

"A solid rock is not disturbed by the wind; even so, a wise person is not agitated by praise or blame." —Dhammapada

"The test of first-rate intelligence is the ability to hold two opposed ideas in the mind at the same time." —F. Scott Fitzgerald

"We don't get harmony when everybody sings the same note. Only notes that are different can harmonize. The same is true with people." —Steve Goodier

"You can't build a relationship with a hammer." —Anonymous

"All conflict we experience in the world is a conflict within our own selves." —Brenda Shoshanna

EXTENSION ACTIVITY

What Would You Do?

What Would You Do? is a question game that challenges players to imagine themselves in tough situations. For this version of the game, the prompts should focus on conflicts. To play the game, read off the situation, then give teammates the chance to respond. You can have players vote on certain actions multiple-choice style in a poll, or call on players to share answers out loud.

Some example prompts:
- What would you do if two teammates refused to speak to each other and used you as an in between?
- What would you do if your boss took credit for your work during a meeting?
- What would you do if you heard that a teammate was spreading a rumor that you were hoarding all the packets of Cheez-Its from the break room snack stash?
- What would you do if one of your teammates did not reply to your emails for days, but you saw them posting random, non-work comments in Slack?

The prompts can be funny, serious, or a mix of both. Players can answer individually; however, you should take the decisions out as a group and have teammates give reasons for or against taking actions. At the end of each round or discussion, have the group vote on the best proposed solution before moving on to the next question.

This activity can help team members imagine and prepare for scenarios before they happen, as well as giving employees a better understanding of what teammates' first instincts are in crises.

SUMMARY QUESTIONS

- How do the stories and/or videos help you handle conflict?
- What other learnings can be gleaned from these stories/videos?
- How do these stories/videos connect to your organization's values?

BIBLIOGRAPHY

Brinkman, Richard & Kirschner, Richard. (1994). *Dealing with People You Can't Stand.* New York: McGraw Hill.
Brown, Brené. (2012). *Daring Greatly.* New York: Penguin.
Crawshaw, Laura. (2007). *Taming the Abrasive Manager.* San Francisco: Jossey-Bass
David, Susan. (2016). *Emotional Agility.* New York: Penguin.
Forward, Susan. (1997). *Emotional Blackmail.* New York: HarperCollins Publishers
Goldsmith, Marshall. (2015). *Triggers.* New York: Crown.
Gottman, John. (1994). *Why Marriages Succeed or Fail.* New York: Fireside
Holiday, Ryan. (2016). *Ego Is the Enemy.* New York: Penguin.
Horn, Sam. (1996). *Tongue Fu.* New York: St. Martin's Griffin.
Horn, Sam. (2004). *Tongue Fu! At School.* Lanham, MD: Rowman & Littlefield.
Johnson, Barry. (1992). *Polarity Management.* Amherst, MA: HRD Press, Inc.
Johnson, Barry. (2020). *And: Making a Difference by Leveraging Polarity, Paradox or Dilemma.* Volume one. Sacramento, CA: Polarity Partnerships.
Joni, S. & Beyer, D. (2010). *The Right Fight.* New York: HarperCollins.
Kashdan, Todd B. (2022). *The Art of Insubordination.* New York: Penguin Random House LLC.
Lynch, Dudley & Kordis, Paul. (1988). *Strategy of the Dolphin.* New York: Fawcett-Columbine Books.
Pink, Daniel. (2009). *Drive.* New York: Riverhead.
Rosenberg, Marshall. (2003). *Nonviolent Communication.* Encinitas, CA: PuddleDancer Press.
Starr, Joshua. (2022). *Equity-Based Leadership: Leveraging Complexity to Transform School Systems.* Cambridge, MA: Harvard.
Waldiner, Robert & Schulz, Marc. (2023). *The Good Life: Lessons from the World's Longest Scientific Study of Happiness.* New York: Simon & Schuster.

Chapter 7

Creativity

"Creativity is more important than knowledge."

—Albert Einstein

WHY THIS TOPIC?

Status quo is not going to be enough for students, colleagues, or the community. Education's mission is to prepare students for life after high school. Physical and psychological safety are the basics for learning. The why, how, and what of learning must continue to evolve. Educators will be required to teach differently for kids who learn differently.

Irvin Studin (2021) writes about three buckets of kids:

1. Kids who learn in traditional school with a teacher.
2. Kids who learn via technology and don't need a lot of outside help.
3. Kids who don't learn in either of the first two ways.

What are the approaches we will use to engage and retain third bucket kids? The number of students in the third bucket is increasing. Without a relationship with those students, educators have no influence with them. Maintaining connections will become more and more important.

In many businesses and industries, creativity is the lifeblood of the organizations. Think about Google, Apple, Pixar, Microsoft, Amazon, and so on. These companies are continually on the lookout for non-traditional learners who see the same information and see new possibilities.

QUOTES TO START CONVERSATIONS

"Vulnerability is the birthplace of innovation, creativity, and change." —Brené Brown

"The worst enemy to creativity is self-doubt." —Sylvia Plath

"You can't use up creativity, the more you use, the more you have." —Maya Angelou

"A mind is like a parachute. It doesn't work if it is not open." —Frank Zappa

"Creativity is as important as literacy." —Ken Robinson

STORIES

The following inventions/discoveries almost didn't happen! It took curiosity, a person(s) who wanted to understand a problem better, and the persistence to find a solution. As we examine the stories of these inventions, we wonder where was the spark of realization when the creators knew they were onto something! How do you harness the power of imagination to fuel your creativity and support your team?

Here are three examples of creative solutions that merged processes from one area to be incorporated in solving an issue.

Story from the Field
By Bill Sommers

A principal, early in his first year, heard the assistant principal say, "Too bad so many kids will drop out this year." The principal asked for clarification. The assistant said we have about 250 dropouts each year. *What*? What is happening here that causes so many kids to leave high school? The assistant said, "It is always that way." The principal looked at the data and found the assistant was accurate: 250–275 students were dropping out each year.

As the conversation continued with the assistant principal during the fall and winter, they discussed what had been tried, some successes, and several failures. There was an alternative program that was working for about 100 students, but they weren't dropping out. The principal noticed that ninth grade was where 75 percent of the problem occurred. Ninety-five percent of juniors went on to graduate as seniors. The principal asked if there were five to six teachers who would be good to work with incoming ninth graders. The assistant found teachers who were willing and committed to keeping kids in school.

The principal met with the six teachers, asked for a commitment from them and gave them a commitment to support them with training, coaching, and team time. In April, the six teachers, the principal, ten community members, and eighty-five ninth grade students met for a day in a neighborhood center. The principal asked the students to tell him and the adults what would keep next year's ninth graders in school and what was keeping them in school. They said having the same teachers all year long, being able to get answers to questions they had like how to manage a checkbook, how to shop for insurance, how to budget their money, and how to manage relationships. The 100 people created a school within a school.

The students who helped plan this new approach became mentors for the incoming ninth graders. The staff had 5 of 6 hours to plan their curriculum as a block. The ninth graders had 1 hour to be in electives. The dropout rate was reduced by 50 percent in 1 year. More kids were connected to the staff. What we didn't anticipate was the huge increase in parent support and positive reinforcement at home.

The Rest of the Story

The demands from a changing world continue to increase. The resources to meet those demands continue to lag behind what is needed. Attempts to increase time on task, school day, school year, and doing more of the same have not kept pace nor shown the dramatic results promised. Of course, like anything, there are pockets of innovation where we can see improvement.

It is time to find additional solutions when what we are doing isn't getting the results we want. To borrow from an Apple ad: think differently.

What we have learned in a combined total of over 140 years in education is, "If it isn't working, try something else." The following are a few strategies to help generate new approaches to add to the repertoire of learning strategies.

Consider This Action #1: Getting to Plan B

In Mullins and Komisar's (2009) book, they write that everyone wants their Plan A to work. And sometimes it does. The most successful individuals and organizations are able to respond when Plan A doesn't work. Think about it, Google founders were searching for a way to organize information. Max Levchin found PayPal on Plan G. Modeling what you do, when you don't know what to do, is great learning for staff and students.

1. What is your Plan A?
2. What will be your Plan B if Plan A doesn't work?
3. Start working on Plan C, and so on. Nothing works all the time.

Velcro
Adaptation by Bill Sommers

George DeMaestral was an engineer in Switzerland. After hunting with his dog in the 1940s, he noticed the cockleburrs in the dog's hair. He had a difficult time trying to remove the burrs. Every time George tried to remove the burrs it seemed that the burr held tight. The burrs were uncomfortable for the dog and very hard to get brush out. George decided to find out why these burrs were so hard to remove.

When looking at the burr and the dog hair under a microscope, George observed there were tiny hooks at the end of the spires from the burr. Voila, he replicated the tiny hooks onto cloth and velcro was born. Thank you George, you have saved many children and adults a lot of work lacing, tying, and strapping.

Post-It Notes
Adaptation by Bill Sommers

Over 90 percent of new ideas fail. Some just don't do what is promised, some because people won't try new ideas, and sometimes people just don't know about the new invention or possible uses. Spencer Silver, in the late 1960s, was working on a new adhesive at 3M. It was supposed to be strong. This adhesive failed.

Art Fry also worked at 3M. He sang in the church choir. He would mark his hymnal with little pieces of paper. Many times as Art turned the pages, the small pieces of paper would fall on the floor. Argh!

Spencer told people about his invention. An adhesive that was not strong and pressure sensitive. By the 1970s, Spencer and Art were talking and a manager thought this might be an answer to a problem. There was little interest shown by top executives. They sent samples out to stores. Not much happened. The product just sat in stores. Not many saw the potential.

Before giving up, the marketing executive sent out free samples to companies. Ninety percent of the companies reordered. The rest is history. Post-Its became a major source of revenue for 3M which, by the way, started as a small sandpaper company in Minnesota.

The Orange and the Sistersmode
Adapted by Bill Sommers

There were two sisters who lived together well into their 80s. Even though they lived in the same house, shared expenses, and basically loved each other, occassionally they would fight over some things. To an outside observer, the issue may seem petty. To the sisters, it was war.

One day they had finished dinner and they saw one orange on the table. Each wanted that orange for dessert. They start bickering over who would get the orange. Both demanded they would get the orange. Finally, a solution: They would cut the orange in half.

One sister removed the peel and ate the succulent fruit inside. The other sister peeled her orange, did not eat the fruit inside but used the peel to make frosting for a cake she was baking.

Discussion Questions

- First, decide what the goal is. Do you want the fruit or the peel for another use?
- Have you ever wasted time and energy fighting over something to later find out you could have solved the dilemma another way?
- Have you ever developed a creative solution to a problem? What happened?
- What were the components to creating a new way of solving a problem? What would you use again? What would you eliminate?
- Who else can help you with coming up with creative solutions? Who are the people you trust the most?

Add your own questions/reflections:

1.
2.
3.
4.
5.

VIDEOS

Students "Outsmart" the Professors (45 seconds)

https://www.youtube.com/watch?v=j-_V_2UzsW0

This video sets up a discussion that students are sometimes more adaptable than staff. Arrogance of a teacher can cause creativity on the part of the students.

Discussion Questions

- Have you ever been out maneuvered by a student, colleague, or supervisor?
- What other creative solution could you have done to retain some power in the relationship?

- Who is/are the best creative thinker(s) you know?
- What can you learn from them?

Add your own questions/reflections:

1.
2.
3.
4.
5.

Ingenious Pot Hole Repair (1:30 minutes)

https://www.youtube.com/watch?v=kYiEfGOqTH8

Someone has to explain to me who designs these things. Not only is this machine cost efficient but time efficient as well. What is the process to generate new solutions to perennial problems? How do we teach this?

Discussion Questions

- Have you ever had an idea you thought was good but nobody else picked up on the possibilities?
- What did you do to either demonstrate the options or change your approach?
- Who are your trusted advisors who will give you true feedback? Make suggestions for improvement?

Add your own questions/reflections:

1.
2.
3.
4.
5.

Armless Tailor (3 minutes)

https://biggeekdad.com/2017/07/the-armless-tailor/

Don't tell me "it can't be done." This amazing video shows a man with no arms who uses his feet to be a tailor. It is being done.

Discussion Questions

- Have you ever had a physical or emotional issue that stopped you from performing normal tasks?
- What did you do to overcome the limitations?
- Who helped you through the time of limiting performance?

Add your own questions/reflections:

1.
2.
3.
4.
5.

QUOTES TO PROMOTE CREATIVITY

"Kids know more ways to learn than we know how to teach." —Bill Sommers

"Turn your future hindsight into your current foresight." —Armen Shirvanian

"If there is a book that you want to read, but it hasn't been written yet, you must be the one to write it." —Toni Morrison

"We drive into the future using only our rear view mirror." —Marshall McLuhan

"'There is something about human curiosity that cannot be hemmed in,' she told me. 'It will find a way to persist, to ask, to question.'" —Amna Khalid

"It's good to be curious about many things." —Mr. Rogers

"Intelligence is something we are born with. Thinking is a skill that must be learned." —Edward de Bono

"It is impossible to live without failing at something unless you live so cautiously that you might as well not have lived at all, in which case you have failed by default." —J.K. Rowling

"If your actions inspire others to dream more, learn more, do more, and become more, you are a leader." —John Quincy Adams

"I am always doing that which I cannot do, in order that I may learn how to do it." —Pablo Picasso

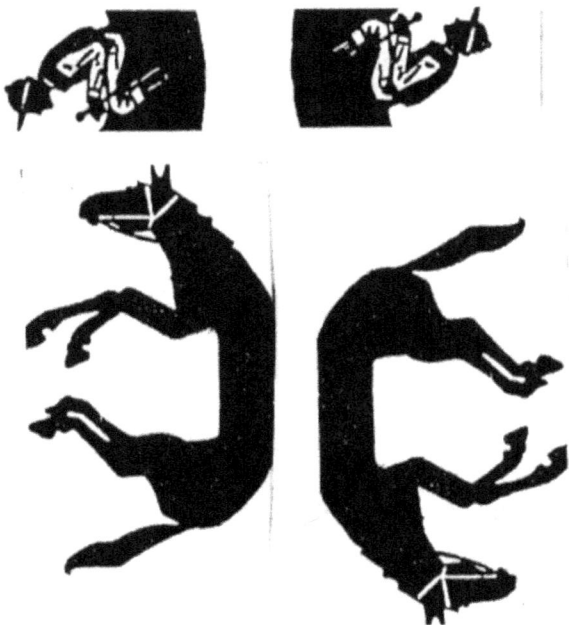

Figure 7.1. Horse and Rider.

EXTENSION ACTIVITY

Using figure 7.1, cut out the four sections. The goal is to have the rider on the horse upright on the horse. It takes a while for one group to find a way. Once one group finds a way to get the riders on the horses, have them help/coach other teams. The answer then spreads through the group.

Activity: The Three Whys

Think of an action by a team member, a car that cut you off in traffic, a partner, or another event that irritated you. The task is to identify three "why did they do that?" questions.

- Example: I was cut off by a car that merged into my lane, almost causing me an accident.
- Y#1—What is why one? He is a schmuck.
- Y#2—What is why two? He has just found out his partner is in the hospital and is rushing to be by their side.
- Y#3—What is why three? He has been late to work on several occasions. The boss has said the next time he is late, he is fired.

SUMMARY QUESTIONS

- How do the stories and/or videos help you make the case for change?
- What other learnings can be gleaned from these stories/videos?
- How do these stories/videos connect to your organization's values?

BIBLIOGRAPHY

Adams, James. (2001). *Conceptual Blockbusting*, 4th ed. New York: Basic Books.
Bock, Lazlo. (2015). *Work Rules.* New York: Twelve.
Briceño, Eduardo. (2023). *The Performance PARADOX: Turning the Power of Mindset into Action.* New York: Ballantine Books.
Catmull, Ed. (2014). *Creativity, Inc.* New York: Random House.
Chaleff, Ira. (2015). *Intelligent Disobedience.* Oakland: Berrett-Koehler.
Gladwell, Malcolm. (2008). *Outliers.* New York: Little, Brown and Company.
Hastings, Reed & Meyer, Erin. (2020). *No Rules Rules.* New York: Penguin.
Heath, Chip & Heath, Dan. (2017). *The Power of Moments.* New York: Simon & Schuster.
Kim, W.C. & Mauborgne, R. (2005). *Blue Ocean Strategy.* Cambridge, MA: Harvard Business School Press.
Kim, W.C. & Mauborgne, R. (2017). *Blue Ocean Shift.* New York: Hachette Books.
Nadler, G. & Hibino, S. (1990). *Breakthrough Thinking.* Rocklin: Prima Publishing & Communications.
Rath, Toma & Conchie, Barry. (2008). *Strengths-Based Leadership.* New York: Gallup Press.
Saphier, Jon. (2017). *High Expectations Teaching.* Thousand Oaks, CA: Corwin Press.
Von Oech, Roger. (1983). *A Whack on the Side of the Head.* New York: Warner Books.
Von Oech, Roger. (2002). *Expect the Unexpected or You Won't Find It.* San Francisco: Berrett-Koehler.
Studin, Irvin. (2021). "Third Bucket Kids and the Future of the Post-Pandemic World." *The Institute for 21st Century Questions.* Retrieved September 24, 2024, from https://www.i21cq.com/publications/third-bucket-kids-and-the-future-of-the-post-pandemic-world/ss.
Wagner, Tony. (2008). *The Global Achievement Gap.* New York: Basic Books.

Chapter 8

Conclusion

Give 'em "L" (Leadership)

"Leadership is action, not position."

—Harold "Bud" Boughton

WHAT DO WE DO NOW?

Here are four possibilities to consider when not much is happening and we know change is needed. These are based on the book *The Knowing-Doing Gap* by Pfeffer and Sutton (2000):

- *When Talk Substitutes for Action*—Talk might feel good but won't lead to doing something positive. Try something, if it works, keep doing it. If it doesn't work, try something else. As Richard Sheridan, CEO of Menlo, says, "run the experiment." See what happens.
- *When Memory Substitutes for Thinking*—Sometimes we have fears from the past, worried about the future that will bring the same results, and we are having feelings in the present. Consider what didn't work in the past, or what parts that didn't work might work now based on changing times and conditions. Times change, people change, and the world is changing.
- *When Fear Prevents Acting on Knowledge*—Fear can freeze people from taking positive steps. W. Edwards Deming said years ago (I paraphrase), "Drive fear out of the organization. Your organization is getting 100 percent congruence with what it is designed to do. If you want different results, look at the design of the organization and quit blaming people."
- *When Measurement Obstructs Good Judgment*—Trust the judgment of the teacher in the classroom who knows the student well. They observe and work with him/her rather than only a test score. They can tell you strengths

and challenges of their students. Relationships and relevance always trump regurgitation.

How do we overcome this knowing-doing gap? Here are a few ways that will help:

- Be clear about why we are doing things the way we do. Are we getting the results we want? If not, try something else. Unleash the potential of your students, colleagues, schools, and community.
- Find out what is working and do more of it. Have a real PLC where the dialogue and exchange of ideas add repertoire, not only a silver bullet that doesn't exist. We need multiple silver bullets for the diversity of life.
- Try something. See what happens. Then adjust or try something else. Ask the students for feedback on what is working for them.
- If you don't want to make mistakes, you probably aren't into learning. Fear of making a mistake will stop some really good ideas. It might be exactly what some person needs to be productive.
- Take fear, guilt, and shame out of learning. None of those three help learning. Read Brené Brown's work on shame. Outstanding.
- Beware of false analogies appearing real—fight the competition, not each other. Confirmation bias and attribution error are deadly to learning.
- Measure what makes the most sense. Content acquisition on a test is one assessment. It is probably not the best indicator of continuing learning potential. Being learning agile is going to pay off in the long run for an ever-changing world.
- Where do leaders spend their time? The killer "Bs"—budgets, buses, and boundaries? Or the lively "Ls"—learning, leading, and lasting relationships?

We also suggest that you start watching Gabor Maté's videos about trauma on YouTube. His books are also very helpful as our world becomes more and more divided, negative, and threatening. Let us know what you think of his ideas. His work on trauma could help educators change the world.

> "You can't write the next chapter of your life if you keep rereading the previous one."
>
> —Marshall Goldsmith

We close with a quote from Seneca written about 2000 years ago:

What gives me pleasure in learning something is that I can teach it. Nothing will ever please me, not even what is remarkably beneficial, if I have learned it for myself only. If wisdom were given to me with this proviso, that I should keep it shut up in myself and never express it to anyone else, I should refuse it: no good is enjoyable to possess without a companion. So I will send you the books themselves; and I will annotate them too, so that you need not expend much effort hunting through them for the profitable bits, but can get right away to the things that I endorse and am impressed with.

A final quote from Angeles Arrien, who has since passed, said years ago,

If your job is waking up the dead, *get up today is a workday*!

QUOTES TO PONDER

"Play is our brain's favorite way of learning." —Diane Ackerman

"A wises teacher makes learning a joy." —Proverbs 15:2

"Life is either a daring adventure or nothing." —Helen Keller

"The sky is the limit." —Amelia Earhart

"The true sign of intelligence is not knowledge but imagination." —Albert Einstein

"The reasonable man adapts himself to the world around him; the unreasonable one persists in trying to adapt the world to himself. Therefore all progress depends on the unreasonable man." —George Bernard Shaw

"You can't solve problems with the same kind of thinking that got you into it." —Albert Einstein

"Never mistake motion for action." —Ernest Hemingway

"Learning never exhausts the mind." —Leonardo Divinci

"If you are not willing to learn, no one can help you. If you are determined to learn, no one can stop you." —Anonymous

"Learning is never cumulative, it is a movement of knowing that has no beginning or end." —Bruce Lee

EXTENSION ACTIVITY

Three Charts

1. Go back 5 years and write down what was hot at the time.
2. What was hot 5 years ago that is still on the top today?
3. What is hot *now* that you think will still be hot in 5 years?

SUGGESTIONS FOR FURTHER STUDY

- "Leadership," Big Think—https://bigthink.com/leadership/.
- Let It Ripple—https://www.letitripple.org/about. Let it Ripple is a 501c3 social profit (nonprofit) known for our global art activations, award-winning films, original series, and live and virtual experiences that inspire audiences to think about what it means to be human in today's world.
- Through Women's Eyes—https://throughwomenseyes.org/.

BIBLIOGRAPHY

Akbar, Maysa. (2020). *Beyond Ally.* Hartford, CT: Publish Your Purpose Press.
Angelou, Maya. (2020). *Pocket Maya Angelou Wisdom.* Hardie Grant Books.
Badaracco, Joseph. (2016). *Managing in the Gray.* Boston: Harvard Business Press.
Barker, Eric. (2017). *Barking Up the Wrong Tree.* New York: HarperCollins.
Block, Peter. (2009). *Community: The Structure of Belonging.* San Francisco: Berrett-Koehler Publishing, Co.
Briceño, Allison & Rodriquez-Mojica, Claudia. (2022). *Conscious Classrooms: Using Diverse Texts for Inclusion, Equity, and Justice.*
Briceño, Eduardo. (2023). *The Performance PARADOX: Turning the Power of Mindset into Action.* New York: Ballantine Books.
Costa, Arthur & Kallick, Bena. (2009). *Habits of Mind across the Curriculum.* Alexandria, VA: ASCD. *(Thinking skills for now and the future.)*
Dintersmith, Ted. (2018). *What School Could Be.* Princeton, NJ: Princeton University Press.
Edmondson, Amy. (2023). *Right Kind of Wrong: The Science of Failing Well.* New York: Atria.
Goldsmith, Marshall. (2007). *What Got You Here Won't Get You There.* New York: Hyperion. *(Goldsmith has written multiple books on leadership and life.)*
Goldsmith, Marshall. (2009). *Mojo.* New York: Hyperion.
Grant, Adam. (2016). *Originals: How Non-Conformists Move the World.* New York: Viking.

Hansen, Ulcca. (2021). *The Future of Smart: How Our Education System Needs to Change to Help All Young People Thrive.* York, PA: Capucia.

Hargreaves, Andy & O'Connor, Michael. (2018). *Collaborative Professionalism.* Thousand Oaks: Corwin Press. *(If Hargreaves writes it, READ IT.)*

Heath, Chip & Heath, Dan. (2017). *The Power of Moments.* New York: Simon & Schuster.

Helgesen, Sally & Goldsmith, Marshall. (2018). *How Women Rise.* New York: Hachette Books.

Helgesen, Sally. (2023). *Rising Together: How We Can Bridge Divides and Create a More Inclusive Workplace.* New York: Hachette.

Johnson, Barry. (2020). *And: Making a Difference by Leveraging Polarity, Paradox or Dilemma.* Volume one. Sacramento, CA: Polarity Partnerships.

Johnson, Stefanie. (2020). *Inclusify.* New York: HarperCollins.

Kleiber, Jenn. (2019). *Building a Bridge from "I Can't" to "I Did!"* USA: Self-Publish.

Livesay, John. (2022). *The Sale Is in the Tale.* Los Angeles: Tradecraft Books.

Mackesy, Charlie. (2019). *The Boy, the Mole, the Fox, and the Horse.* New York: HarperCollins.

Maté, Gabor, MD with Maté, Daniel. (2022). *The Myth of Normal.* New York: Penguin Random House.

Olsen, Skip & Sommers, William. (2004) *A Trainer's Companion: Stories for Conversations, Reflection, and Action.* Baytown, TX: AhaProcess, Inc.

Palmer, Parker. (1998). *The Courage to Teach.* San Francisco, CA: Jossey-Bass.

Pink, Daniel. (2022). *The Power of Regret.* New York: Riverhead Books.

Reynolds, Jason & Kendi, Ibram. (2020). *Stamped: Racism, Antiracism, and You.* New York: Little, Brown and Company.

Rios, Victor & Mireles-Rios, Rebeca. (2019). *My Teacher Believes in Me! The Educator's Guide to At-Promise Students.* Five Rivers Press.

Ryan, Tony. (2018). *The Next Generation.* Melbourne, Australia: Wiley.

Saphier, Jon. (2017). *High Expectations Teaching.* Thousand Oaks, CA: Corwin Press. *(Our go-to guru on learning: Research for Better Teaching.)*

Sarsour, Linda. (2020). *We Are Not Here to be Bystanders.* New York: Simon and Schuster.

Sheridan, Richard. (2018). *Chief Joy Officer.* New York: Portfolio/Penguin.

Sutton, Robert & Rao, Huggy. (2014). *Scaling Up Excellence.* New York: Crown Publishing.

Appendix

Three Things to Know About Copyright Laws When Using Video

INTRODUCTION

If a picture is worth a thousand words, then a video is priceless. Using video as a teaching tool brings ideas to life and stimulates interest in learners. Today, we have access to more video content than any other time in history. Capitalizing on this wealth of information requires diligent planning to ensure proper use of someone's creative material, especially if a teacher uses video in a public setting. Often educators erroneously believe that video streamed from the internet can be used in classrooms or professional learning without violating copyright laws. Here are the top three things you need to know about using video as a teaching tool:

- how to use online video legally (copyright laws for using video with students and adults)
- tips for searching for a copyright owner
- how to obtain permission to use video legally

WHAT ARE THE RULES FOR USING VIDEO LEGALLY (COPYRIGHT LAWS FOR USING VIDEO WITH STUDENTS AND ADULTS)

Often as educators we learn the phrase, "fair use." Sometimes we believe that because we are using video as a teaching tool, that we have the privilege of sharing streamed video without obtaining permission. What does "fair use" really mean? "Fair use" provides for "freedom of expression by permitting

Appendix

Table A.1.

IF	Then
The video is used in a commercial nature (for profit)	• Obtain permission in writing prior to use of video material • Negotiate an agreement to use a specified portion of video
The video is used for nonprofit educational purposes	• Obtain permission in writing prior to use of video material • It is best if the use is "transformative," adds something new to the original work, and does not infringe on the owner's financial profit • Example: Sometimes parodies are viewed by courts as transformative • Example: Short film clips used in a biography may be considered transformative because they are used for a different purpose than the original film[1]
The work used is of a creative or imaginative nature	• Obtain permission in writing prior to use of video material or refrain from using the video • Novels, songs, or movies are less likely to qualify as "fair use" because they are of a creative nature
The work used is factual, technical, or news related	• Obtain permission in writing prior to use of copyrighted video material • Factual material is more likely to be considered "fair use" for educators • Using an unpublished work is frequently considered "fair use"
A short portion of the video is selected for use	• Obtain permission in writing prior to use of copyrighted material • A short portion is more likely considered "fair use" • Even a short clip that contains the "heart" of the work may infringe on the copyright owner's rights[2]
A longer portion or the entire video is selected for use	• Obtain permission in writing prior to use of copyrighted material • A longer portion or the entire video is less likely to be considered "fair use"
The copyright owner's potential market may be impacted by your use	• Obtain permission in writing prior to use of copyrighted material • If the owner loses sales, "fair use" does not apply • Consider the consequences if the use becomes widespread[3]

[1] Justia Legal Resources. (2021, October 18). *Transformative Use and Copyright Infringement.* Justia. Retrieved August 28, 2022, from https://www.justia.com/intellectual-property/copyright/fair-use/transformative-use/.
[2] YouTube, T. of S. (2022). *Fair Use on YouTube—YouTube Help.* Google. Retrieved August 31, 2022, from https://support.google.com/youtube/answer/9783148?hl=en&ref_topic=2778546#zippy=%2Cthe-purpose-and-character-of-the-use-including-whether-such-use-is-of-commercial-nature-or-is-for-non-profit-educational-purposes%2Cthe-amount-and-substantiality-of-the-portion-used-in-relation-to-the-copyrighted-work-as-a-whole.
[3] Driskill, E., Moore, J., & Cano, L. (2022, June 30). *Copyright Rules of Using Video.* Personal.

unlicensed use of copyright-protected works in certain circumstances."[1] See table A.1 to understand the nuance of "fair use," and potential next steps for using video publicly.[2]

GUIDELINES FOR USING VIDEO IN PUBLIC PRESENTATIONS

1. *Select a video* you are interested in using. Ask permission anytime you plan to use any video you did not personally create and get permission in writing. In order to obtain permission from the copyright owner, it is recommended to use a shortened portion of the video.
2. *Ensure you allow enough time* for communication with the video owner. Using video without permission is essentially stealing another artist's creative property. Ask permission anytime you plan to use any video you did not personally create and get permission to use the video in writing. It can be time consuming.
3. *Locate the copyright owner* of the selected video. Often videos and video clips are posted on the internet by individuals who do not own the copyright to the content that they post. While YouTube works to remove these videos, the content can be reposted under a different name quickly and easily. It often requires searching layer by layer to obtain the name of the company or individual and the means to contact for permission.
4. *Link to the owner's site or channel* rather than downloading the video when using video for a public performance. Downloading the video is similar to copying music to play without paying streaming fees or obtaining a license for public performance. In order to play a video publicly, you must have a legally obtained copy.
5. *Maintain accurate records* that demonstrate attempts to obtain permission to use a video and the responses received in response to your requests.
6. *Use the same guidelines for presentations with students in school,* however, after you have asked permission to use a video, the "fair use" clause may provide more leniency if used for an educational purpose.
7. *Find Creative Commons or Public Domain videos* for use. Videos in these categories may sometimes be used in the entirety without any alteration if you give attribution. Videos on YouTube marked with Creative Commons license allow anyone to reuse the video or edit it.[3] Some websites offer free video stock footage for use. See our helpful links section for a few options.

TIPS FOR SEARCHING FOR COPYRIGHT OWNER

Video clips can be used with written permission via a letter or email. It can feel like a scavenger hunt to locate the owner/creator of online videos. Find the owner by looking in the YouTube description, credits, or channel information. Frequently, the description will give licensing information and credits. It will also give information about how to get to the channel. Access the channel information on YouTube, and the details section will sometimes provide an email address for business inquiry.

When using a video from a website other than YouTube, you may need to contact a webmaster or page owner. When the owner has been located and a website obtained, look for a contact us, permissions, outreach page, copyright notice, or legal notice to find contact information.

If the video is posted on social media, make contact via the social media platform message system.[4] Persistence is the key to locating the creator/owner of the copyright. You will proceed layer by layer to find the creator/owner of the original copyrighted video. Due to a 1989 law, copyright notices are not required. If you are unable to locate a copyright notice, it "does not mean the work may be used without permission, copied, adapted, distributed, or publicly displayed." To further complicate matters, copyright ownership may be sold or transferred after publication, and you will need to contact the current owner. See "Helpful Links" for the link to Copyright Public Records Portal.

HOW TO OBTAIN PERMISSION TO USE VIDEO

Allow ample time to contact a copyright owner prior to using their creative work. Delays in granting permission are often the result of inaccurate or incomplete information given to the copyright owner. You will need the following information to request permission to use a video in presentations. This form may be copied for your use to request permission.

REQUEST FOR PERMISSION TO USE COPYRIGHTED VIDEO

Video author's, editor's, or translator's full name _____

Video title _____

Additional details about the work (example: edition or volume number)

___

Request to use which portion of the video (include start and end time in minutes and seconds) (You may want to include a description of the clip.)

___

___

___

Copyright date of the video___

Describe in detail how the video will be used (date(s), purpose, how it will be edited or not, how frequently you are requesting to use the video, how the video will be shared with the audience (public performance, Learning Management System, online learning etc.))

___

___

___

___

___

Audience who will participate in the public presentation

___

Will the video be included in a product to be sold? Describe

___

___

___

Name of organization making the request ___

What is the nature of the organization making the request (non-profit, for-profit)?

___

Person or organization requesting to use the video

Full name ___

Email ___

Address ___

Phone ___

HELPFUL LINKS

- Fair use on YouTube—https://support.google.com/youtube/answer/9783148?hl=en&ref_topic=2778546.
- Free stock video footage:
  - https://www.videvo.net/—Videvo provides free stock video footage, sound effects, and music tracks. Some are royalty free and others require attribution.
  - Movieclips.com.
- Copyright Clearance Center's Motion Picture License—https://www.copyright.com/solutions-motion-picture-license/. This site provides licensed access to show scenes and full-length movies and TV shows at sales meetings, employee trainings, and company functions.
- Copyright Public Records Portal—https://www.copyright.gov/public-records/.
- Copyright Records from January 1, 1978 to the present—https://www.copyright.gov/.
- Copyright Registrations, Moving Image Archive—https://archive.org/details/movies.
- Potential license for using video or services to obtain legal use of video—https://www.copyright.gov/circs/m10.pdf.

NOTES

1. https://www.copyright.gov/fair-use/index.html. Last updated June 2022.
2. US Copyright Office. (2013). *How to Obtain Permission.* Copyright.gov. Retrieved July 12, 2022, from https://www.copyright.gov/circs/m10.pdf.
3. YouTube, T. of S. (2022). *Creative Commons—YouTube Help.* Google. Retrieved August 31, 2022, from https://support.google.com/youtube/answer/2797468#.
4. Rubin, J. (2013, May 4). *Video Copyright: How to Avoid Getting Sued.* Digital.gov. Retrieved August 31, 2022, from https://digital.gov/2013/05/04/video-copyright/.

Contact Information

HOW CAN WE ASSIST YOU?

Learning Omnivores: https://learningomnivores.com/
Lian Dante Foundation: https://www.liandantefoundation.org/
Margie Blount: Linkedin
Elita Driskill: Linkedin

Index

Page references for figures are italicized

Adair, Lara, 69–70

Bar of Soap Story, 21–24
Block, Peter, 77
Blount, Margie, 118
Brown, Brené, 1–2
Bury My Heart at Conference Room B, 3–5

Chadwick, Bob, 80–82
change, 63–75
Chicken Soup for the Grieving Soul. See I Wish You Enough story
coaching, 47–61
Coaching Versus Telling story, 51–52
collaboration, 33–46
The Collaboration Cycle story, 39
communication, 17–32
Communities of Practice, 66–67
community, 65–66
conflict, 77–87
copyright laws and permissions for videos, 105–10
courage, 1–15
creativity, 89–97
Cross Your Arms activity, 74

Depends on Your Perspective story, 80–82
Driskill, Elita, 118–19

Empowered Management, 77
Ernest Shackleton story, 7–9
essential coaching skills for strong leadership, 47–48

Florence Taylor story, 3–5
Force-Field Analysis activity, 73–74
Four Kinds of Power story, 49–51
Fulp, Carol, 35

Gabra story, 5–7
Goldsmith, Marshall, 63–64
Gorilla Story, 67–68

Helgesen, Sally, 49–51
"*How Are the Children?*" story, 37–38
Humble Inquiry story, 53–54

Ideal Team Player diagram, *45*
The Ideal Team Player, 44–45
I Wish You Enough story, 19–20

Jenkins, Ted, 49–51

The Knowing-Doing Gap, 99–100

Last Word: An Improv Exercise, 31
Lencioni, Patrick, 44–45
Livesay, John, 26–28

The Monk's Story, 39–40
Musical Tunes for Change activity, 74

Nonviolent Communication: A Language of Life, 25

O'Neill, Patrick T., 37–38

Perks, Bob, 19–20
Pfeffer, Jeffrey, 99–100
Pollock, Lindsey, *116*, 117
Post-It Notes story, 92
The Power of the Badge story, 79–80
professional conversations, *60*

Rosenberg, Marshall, 25

The Sale Is in the Tale story, 26–28
Schein, Edgar, 53–55
Singer, Tonya Ward, 1–2

Slap, Stan, 3–5
Sommers, 5–7, 115–17
Story from the Field, 90–91
Success through Diversity: Why the Most Inclusive Companies Will Win, 35
Surowiecki, James, 34–35
Sutton, Robert I., 99–100
Switch Places activity, 73

The 10th Step story, 78–79
There Are CATS in Our DOG HOUSE story, 69–70

Values activity, 13–14
Velcro story, 92

Wenger, Etienne, 66–67
The Whale story, 36
What Got You Here Won't Get You There: The Success Delusion, or Why We Resist Change, 63–64
What Would You Do? activity, 86–87
When Children Turn into Cats, 69–70
Windows and Mirrors story, 25–26
The Wisdom of Crowds, 34

About the Authors

Figure D.1. Bill Sommers

William (Bill) A. Sommers has been a consultant for leadership coaching, cognitive coaching, adaptive schools, brain research, poverty, habits of mind, and conflict management. He was also on the board of trustees of the National Staff Development Council (now called Learning Forward) for 5 years and served as president in 2006.

Bill is a certified Stakeholder Centered Coach, certified as a WHY Institute consultant, as well as Leveraging Polarities.

Dr. Sommers is the former executive director for Secondary Curriculum and Professional Learning for Minneapolis Public Schools and has been a school administrator for over 35 years. He has been a senior fellow for the Urban Leadership Academy at the University of Minnesota and has served as an adjunct faculty member at Texas State University, Hamline University,

University of St. Thomas, and St. Mary's University. Bill has been a program director for an adolescent chemical dependency treatment center and on the advisory board of a halfway house for 20 years.

Bill has authored and co-authored over ten books, including:

Stakeholder Centered Coaching for Educators (in press)
Compliance Cop to Culture Coach (2023)
Creating Talent Density: Accelerating Adult Learning (2021)
Responding to Resistance: 30 Ways to Manage Conflict in Schools (2019)
9 Professional Conversations to Change Schools: A Dashboard of Options (2018)
Living on a Tightrope: A Survival Handbook for Principals
Being a Successful Principal: How to Ride the Wave of Change Without Drowning
Reflective Practice to Improve Schools (now in the third edition
    as *Reflective Practice for Renewing Schools*)
A Trainer's Companion: *Stories to Cause Inspiration & Reflection*
Energizing Staff Development Using Video Clips
Leading Professional Learning Communities
Guiding Professional Learning Communities
Principal's Field Manual
Habits of Mind Teacher's Companion (in the second edition)

In January 2016, Bill and his colleague Skip Olsen launched the website www.learningomnivores.com, which includes educational posts, new rules, and book reviews.

Bill has come out of retirement multiple times to put theory into practice in urban, suburban, and rural schools. He is a practitioner who integrates theory

Figure D.2. Lindsey Pollock

into leading and facilitating schools. Dr. Sommers continues to coach school and district leaders as he has done for over 35 years.

Lindsey Pollock, EdD, LCSW, is the current provost of Sarasota University where she oversees education programs founded on Montessori principles. Her passion for education is part of her DNA. She was inspired by the dedication and work ethic of her family: dad (a college professor), mom (a first-grade teacher), grandpa (a school custodian), brother (a college professor), sister (a teaching assistant), and husband (a public school principal). Education is in the family! Her 35+ year career in the field of education has been filled with exciting adventures and keeps her motivated to set new goals!

Dr. Pollock has led private for-profit and non-profit schools as an administrator and owned and managed a small retail business. Dr. Pollock has consulted with schools across the United States and has been an international speaker/consultant to school systems/organizations in Sweden, China, Brazil, Mexico, and Ghana. Dr. Pollock has written numerous articles for national publications and wrote a monthly parenting column for the *Garden Oaks Gazette* for 13 years.

She continues to serve on local, state, and national non-profit boards including Montessori for Social Justice and Texas Education and Advocacy for Montessori. Her dedication to social justice has been recognized by numerous organizations, including the Human Rights Campaign. Dr. Pollock holds a Montessori Administrator credential along with her Texas teaching certifications in elementary education (1st–8th grades), special education (PK–12), English as a second language, speech communications (1st–8th grades), mid-management administrator (PK–12), and superintendent (EC–12). She was chosen as a Rice fellow in the Rice Education Entrepreneurial Program (REEP), represented the United States as a Fulbright Exchange Principal, and attended Harvard with Raise Your Hand Texas for numerous certification programs in Educational Leadership. She earned master's degrees in Montessori integrative learning, educational leadership, and social work as well as a doctorate in educational leadership.

In her free time, she volunteers as the executive director of the Lian Dante Foundation in Houston, Texas, and teaches for the Center for Guided Montessori Studies (CGMS). Her efforts continue to impact classrooms and communities in new and ever-meaningful ways.

Figure D.3. Margie Blount

Margie Blount, EdD, of Katy, Texas, is a teacher, principal, professor, leadership coach, and a consultant for 33 years. Her leadership serves as a catalyst to build and enhance strong relationships within learning communities to ensure the implementation of effective and targeted strategies. Strategies that result in a growth mindset within individuals, foster conflict resolution, improve academic achievement, and support social and emotional well-being for students and educators. These accomplishments encompass leading and strategizing for diverse campuses, recruiting highly qualified staff, fostering a positive school culture, and implementing data-driven instructional leadership in both rural and suburban districts. Her skill set extends to coaching educators, program monitoring and evaluation, and building strong relationships with team members, parents, and community stakeholders. She has extensive experience in team building, collaborative planning, and developing effective leaders.

She earned a Bachelor of Arts degree in business administration and secondary education and a Master of Education degree in administration from Stephen F. Austin State University. In 2014 she received a Doctorate of Education degree in educational leadership from Lamar University. Additionally, Dr. Blount is a consultant for cognitive coaching, adaptive schools, brain research, habits of mind, conflict management, and classroom management strategies. Margie serves as a field supervisor for the Educational Leadership Program at Lamar University. She serves on the boards of directors for the Lian Dante Foundation and Montessori for Social Justice. Contact Margie on LinkedIn.

Elita Driskill currently serves with Others Centered Solutions LLC as the owner and consultant who focuses on coaching, leadership communication

Figure D.4. Elita Driskill

skills, and team building. She holds certifications as a Texas administrator and teacher, ICF Professional Certified Coach, and Gallup Strength Coach. As a lifelong educator, she taught middle and high school and served as an instructional coach, Education Service Center regional consultant, director of technology integration and innovation, and director of professional learning. Driskill has worked with K–12 preservice teachers, support staff, child nutrition staff, teachers, teacher leaders, administrators, and superintendents. She is the author of several professional articles, blogs, vlogs, and co-author of research articles. In 2008, she became a member of Learning Forward Texas, later served on the board of directors, and now serves as a consultant to provide high-quality professional learning. Because Elita believes that "a wise teacher makes learning a joy," she infuses her work with interaction, laughter, and collaboration. Connect with Elita on LinkedIn.

www.ingramcontent.com/pod-product-compliance
Lightning Source LLC
Chambersburg PA
CBHW051103230426
43667CB00013B/2419